Study Guide
John Bowdidge
George Swales

BUSINESS ESSENTIALS

Ronald J. Ebert
University of Missouri-Columbia

Ricky W. Griffin
Texas A&M University

Prentice Hall, Englewood Cliffs, NJ 07632

Project manager: Amy Hinton
Acquisitions editor: Donald Hull
Manufacturing buyer: Ken Clinton

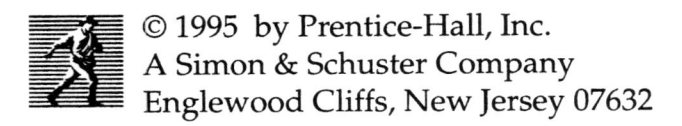

© 1995 by Prentice-Hall, Inc.
A Simon & Schuster Company
Englewood Cliffs, New Jersey 07632

All rights reserved. No part of this book may be
reproduced, in any form or by any means,
without permission in writing from the publisher.

Printed in the United States of America

10 9 8 7 6 5 4 3 2

ISBN 0-13-305756-9

Prentice-Hall International (UK) Limited, *London*
Prentice-Hall of Australia Pty. Limited, *Sydney*
Prentice-Hall Canada Inc., *Toronto*
Prentice-Hall Hispanoamericana, S.A., *Mexico*
Prentice-Hall of India Private Limited, *New Delhi*
Prentice-Hall of Japan, Inc., *Tokyo*
Simon & Schuster Asia Pte. Ltd., *Singapore*
Editora Prentice-Hall do Brasil, Ltda., *Rio de Janeiro*

PREFACE

TO THE STUDENT

A beginning course in business administration has the potential to become, for many students, a decisive factor in determining a career choice. We hope that this study guide will help to make the course even more worthwhile. Here's what you will find in each chapter.

CHAPTER OVERVIEW

This is a quick capsule of what the textbook chapter has to offer. It can never serve as a substitute for reading the entire chapter. But if you get in a hurry, and really want to pick up the essence of a chapter in a few seconds, this overview should serve you well.

LEARNING OBJECTIVES

Ebert and Griffin, in the main textbook, have listed objectives for each chapter. Such a list can serve as your guide in seeking out the salient points and being sure that you have not missed something. For your convenience, we have merely listed these objectives in our study guide.

DISCUSSION OF OPENING VIGNETTE

Each chapter in the textbook will have, among other special features, an opening vignette and a business case. All of these are great! What we offer in our study guide is a glance at the vignette from a slightly different angle. For example, in Chapter 13, the opening vignette tells of a couple of gentlemen who devise a method for sending songs to loved ones on special holidays. Our "discussion" centers first upon the market research aspect of the case. And then we compare the Send-a-Song operation with a concept originally proposed in an old Bing Crosby-Fred Astaire movie called "Holiday Inn." Four fresh questions are offered to spur innovative thinking.

ANNOTATED KEY TERMS

In the margins of your main textbook, you'll find that key terms have been defined. This placement in the margin makes them easy to find. Well, in the study guide, we have listed all of these terms together.

TRUE-FALSE AND MULTIPLE CHOICE QUESTIONS

To help you to review what you have read in a given chapter, ten true-false and twenty multiple choice questions are available in the study guide. Answers for these are found at the very end of each study guide chapter. It's possible that some professors may want to use some of these questions on tests.

WRITING TO LEARN

All across the country and at almost all grade levels, it is being said that students do not have enough opportunities to engage in composition. This study guide can help. With each chapter of the guide, you will find nine topics about which to write. Some of them call for rather extensive crafting of sentences. Some of the suggested topics call for a reciting of what you have learned in reading the textbook chapter, but other topics allow you to roam the creative meadows of your mind. This section can be lots of fun.

DISCUSSION OF THE BUSINESS CASE

Just as with the Opening Vignette, the study guide attacks each case with a totally different slant. If the study guide can add a new dimension to what the book has reported, then the student in the same fashion can easily add additional insights not touched upon by either text or study guide. And, yes, there will be four new questions to open up new thinking about each case.

ANSWERS TO QUESTIONS

Not only have we provided answers to the objective questions on the final page of each chapter, but we have indicated for each the number of the textbook page on which the answer can be found.

TO THE PROFESSOR

We trust that you will find that this study guide is helpful to your students. Professors who discuss the Opening Vignette and/or the Business Case will find that the study guide attempts to provide some new insights as well as additional questions. Since we offer ten true-false questions and twenty multiple choice questions with each of the eighteen chapters, this means we have provided 540 new questions for you to use over this material. For essay questions, you may use the items in the "Writing to Learn" section. With nine such topics per chapter, this provides 135 essay questions. Answers to the essay questions must be supplied by the professor. We hope this study guide will be of help to both teacher and student in the beginning course in business administration.

George S. Swales, Jr.
John S. Bowdidge

CHAPTER ONE

UNDERSTANDING THE U.S. BUSINESS SYSTEM

CHAPTER OVERVIEW

An economic system is a nation's system for allocating its resources among citizens. The basic resources that a business uses to produce goods and services are called factors of production--natural resources, labor, capital, and entrepreneurs. A planned economy--such as socialism or communism--relies on a centralized government to control all or most factors of production. In market economies, individuals (producers and consumers) control production and allocation decisions. Demand is the willingness and ability of buyers to purchase a product. Supply is the willingness and ability of producers to offer a good or service for sale. Private enterprise is a system that allows individuals to pursue their own interests without governmental restriction. Economists have identified four basic degrees of competition: pure competition, monopolistic competition, oligopoly, and monopoly. Nearly every economic system has three broad goals: stability, full employment, and growth. The success of an economic system is judged by one or more of these measures: gross national product, productivity, balance of trade, and national debt. The government attempts to manage the U.S. economy through two sets of policies: monetary and fiscal.

LEARNING OBJECTIVES

1. Define the nature of U.S. business and its goals.

2. Describe different types of economic systems according to the means by which they control the factors of production.

3. Show how demand and supply affect resource distribution in the United States.

4. Identify the elements of private enterprise and explain the various degrees of competition in the U.S. economic system.

5. Explain the criteria for evaluating the success of an economic system meeting its goals and explain how the federal government attempts to manage the U.S. economy.

DISCUSSION OF OPENING VIGNETTE

Talk about the need to be adaptable! When your firm builds its business on "short-lived fads," the management can never rest. At least Topps has an advantage over some other firms. And that is because Topps knows that drastic changes are occurring in the marketplace. Within more settled and stable firms, it is difficult to get company personnel to realize that the presence of change is something that never changes. For example, merchants who operated successful and customer-jammed businesses in the centers of large American cities up through the 1950's believed that conditions downtown would never change. Sure, a minor shopping center would open up out on the edge of town now and then, but that had no impact on those wonderful people who liked the exhilaration of "going to town" to shop. Being blind to the environment, such merchants didn't awake until it was too late. Well, Topps has been awakened to several facts. It is difficult to build a national business around one product, and a seasonal one at that. Diversification is the answer. The downside here is that a firm such as Topps will have to learn further lessons by trial and error. Regardless of how much market research is done in advance, some miscalculations are bound to occur. Topps might try marketing baseball cards in little glass frames--ideal for hanging in a family room! Until they put them on sale, they won't know for sure if they have a hit on their hands. Yes, the marketplace can change and Topps is fully aware of this fact. Forewarned is forearmed.

1. Do you think that Topps' emphases are still too narrow in scope since they all have to do with the broad field of entertainment? Why or why not?

2. What might be some other areas Topps might enter in an effort to provide greater diversification?

3. In light of the Topps case that you have just read, tell what you think of this possible company goal: "We are now going to manufacture the BEST baseball cards in the world!"

4. You are a member of the board of directors at Topps. A staff member comes up with the idea to print cards for: soccer, hockey, girls college softball, professional wrestling, and rock stars. Evaluate the potential success for each of these proposed ventures.

ANNOTATED KEY TERMS

<u>Business</u> - An organization that provides goods or services to earn profits.

<u>Profits</u> - The difference between a business's revenues and its expenses.

<u>Economic system</u> - A nation's system for allocating its resources among its citizens.

<u>Factors of production</u> - Resources used in the production of goods and services--natural resources, labor, capital, and entrepreneurs.

<u>Natural resources</u> - Materials supplied by nature such as land, water, mineral deposits, and trees.

<u>Labor (or human resources)</u> - The mental and physical capabilities of people as they contribute to economic production.

<u>Capital</u> - The funds needed to create and operate a business enterprise.

<u>Entrepreneur</u> - Person who embraces the opportunities and accepts the risks in creating and operating a business.

<u>Planned economy</u> - Economy that relies on a centralized government to control all or most factors of production and to make all or most production and allocation decisions.

<u>Market economy</u> - Economy in which individuals control production and allocation decisions through supply and demand.

<u>Communism</u> - Planned economic system in which the government owns and operates all sources of production.

<u>Socialism</u> - Planned economic system in which the government owns and operates only selected major sources of production.

<u>Market</u> - Mechanism for exchange between buyers and sellers of a particular good or service.

<u>Capitalism</u> - Market economy that provides for private ownership of production and encourages entrepreneurship by offering profit as an incentive.

<u>Mixed market economy</u> - Economy featuring characteristics of both planned and market economies.

<u>Privatization</u> - Process of converting government enterprises into privately owned companies.

<u>Demand</u> - The willingness and ability of buyers to purchase a good or service.

<u>Supply</u> - The willingness and ability of producers to offer a good or service for sale.

<u>Law of demand</u> - Principle that buyers will purchase (demand) more of a product as its price drops and less as its price increases.

<u>Law of supply</u> - Principle that producers will offer (supply) more of a product for sale as its price rises and less as its price drops.

<u>Demand and supply schedule</u> - Assessment of the relationships between different levels of demand and supply at different price levels.

<u>Demand curve</u> - Graph showing how many units of a product will be demanded (bought) at different prices.

<u>Supply curve</u> - Graph showing how many units of a product will be supplied (offered for sale) at different prices.

<u>Equilibrium price (or market price)</u> - Profit-maximizing price at which the quantity of goods demanded and the quantity of goods supplied are equal.

<u>Surplus</u> - Situation in which quantity supplied exceeds quantity demanded.

<u>Shortage</u> - Situation in which quantity demanded exceeds quantity supplied.

<u>Private enterprise</u> - Economic system that allows individuals to pursue their own interests without undue governmental restriction.

<u>Private property</u> - The right to buy, own, use, and sell almost any form of property.

<u>Freedom of choice</u> - The right to choose what to buy or sell, including the individual's right to offer his or her labor.

<u>Competition</u> - Vying among businesses for the same resources or customers.

<u>Pure competition</u> - Market or industry characterized by a very large number of small firms producing an identical product.

<u>Monopolistic competition</u> - Market or industry characterized by (1) a large number of buyers and (2) a relatively large number of sellers trying to differentiate products from those of the competitors.

<u>Oligopoly</u> - Market or industry characterized by a handful of (generally very large) sellers with the power to influence the prices of their products.

Monopoly - Market or industry in which there is only one producer who can therefore set the prices of its products.

Natural monopoly - Industry in which one company can most efficiently supply all needed goods or services.

Stability - Condition in which the balance between the money available in an economy and the goods produced in it remains about the same.

Inflation - Period of widespread price increases throughout an economic system.

Recession - Period characterized by decreases in employment, income, and production.

Depression - Particularly severe and long-lasting recession.

Unemployment - Level of joblessness among people actively seeking work.

Growth - Increase in the amount of goods and services produced by a nation's resources.

Gross national product (GNP) - Total value of all the goods and services produced by an economic system in a one-year period.

Real gross national product - Gross national product adjusted for inflation and changes in the value of a country's currency.

Productivity - Measure of economic growth that compares how much a system produces to the resources needed to produce it.

Balance of trade - Difference between a nation's exports to and imports from other countries.

Budget deficit - Situation in which a government body spends more money in one year than it takes in.

National debt - Total amount that a nation owes to creditors.

Monetary policies - Government economic policies that focus on controlling the size of a nation's money supply.

Fiscal policies - Government economic policies centered on the ways the government collects and spends its revenues.

TRUE-FALSE QUESTIONS

F 1. The factors of production are natural resources, labor, capital, and opportunity.

T 2. Labor includes both the mental and physical capabilities of people as they are engaged in economic production.

F 3. The funds needed to operate an enterprise are referred to as natural resources.

F 4. A market economy relies on a centralized government to control all or most of the factors of production.

F 5. Socialism and communism are similar. Socialism is a system in which the government owns and operates all sources of production, whereas communism is a system in which the government owns and operates only <u>selected</u> industries.

T 6. A mixed market economy features characteristics of both planned and market economies.

F 7. The law of demand states that producers will offer more of a product for sale as its price rises and less as its price drops.

F 8. In pure competition, there are very few sellers.

F 9. In monopolistic competition, just as in pure competition, products of all the sellers are very similar.

T 10. Since the end of World War II, unemployment in the United States has generally varied between 5 and 10 percent.

MULTIPLE CHOICE QUESTIONS

1. It is defined as the condition in which the balance between the money available in an economy and the goods produced in the economy remains about the same. What is it?

   a. stability
   b. inflation
   c. growth
   d. frictional unemployment

2. It is defined as an increase in the amount of goods and services produced by a nation's resources. What is it?

   a. monopoly
   b. productivity
   c. growth
   d. gross national product

3. What governs how a government collects and spends its revenues?

   a. monetary policy
   b. productivity
   c. national debt
   d. fiscal policy

4. Which of the following is NOT a factor of production?

   a. productivity
   b. natural resources
   c. capital
   d. labor

5. Below will be found a term that the textbook says is often substituted for the economic term "labor." Pick it out of the group.

   a. people
   b. resources
   c. human resources
   d. workers

6. "Embrace the opportunities and accept the risks." The preceding phrase relates to--

   a. capital
   b. labor
   c. natural resources
   d. entrepreneurs

7. One of the phrases below is definitely out of place. Which is it?

   a. centralized control
   b. producers control production
   c. planned economy
   d. socialism

8. What do the following nations have in common? China, Cuba, North Korea, and Vietnam.

   a. socialism
   b. mixed economy
   c. market economy
   d. communism

7

9. What do the following nations have in common? Poland, Bulgaria, and Russia.

   a. socialism
   b. mixed economy
   c. market economy
   d. communism

10. It is a process in which control of a firm is taken away from a government. What is it?

   a. privatization
   b. arrested control
   c. socialism
   d. mercantilism

11. It states that buyers will purchase more of a product if its price drops. This is a partial statement of--

   a. supply
   b. law of supply
   c. demand
   d. law of demand

12. On a graph, the point at which the supply curve crosses the demand curve is referred to as--

   a. the junction
   b. the demander's spot
   c. the equilibrium price
   d. the law of demand

13. At the point where the supply curve crosses the demand curve on a graph, it could be said that--

   a. no sales will be made
   b. all products offered for sale will be sold
   c. a shortage will result
   d. a surplus will result

14. In his book Wealth of Nations, Adam Smith maintained that the creation of wealth should be the concern of--

   a. heavenly powers
   b. the government
   c. individuals
   d. students

15. One of the fundamental rights guaranteed by the U.S. Constitution, according to the textbook, is--

   a. the right to own property
   b. the right to make a profit
   c. the right to bankruptcy
   d. the right to put a business building where you please

16. In a given national market, only five firms make and distribute popular red wagons. This illustrates which degree of competition?

 a. oligopoly
 b. pure competition
 c. monopoly
 d. monopolistic competition

17. Individual firms must be small and the number of such firms must be large. This describes which degree of competition?

 a. oligopoly
 b. pure competition
 c. monopoly
 d. monopolistic competition

18. Which of the following is NOT characteristic of an oligopoly?

 a. great product differentiation
 b. few sellers
 c. swift response to price change of a competitor
 d. prices differ greatly

19. Which of the following is NOT offered by the textbook as a goal of an economic system?

 a. stability
 b. full employment
 c. quality
 d. growth

20. Which of the following is mentioned by the book as a measure of economic performance?

 a. productivity
 b. quality
 c. volume
 d. trade potential

WRITING TO LEARN

1. Fully describe the four degrees of competition. Mention characteristics of each and give examples of industries that illustrate each.

2. Explain what is meant by the term "privatization," and then provide a fictional scenario of a privatization taking place.

3. Consider the Russian Republic today and explain what kind of economy you think it has. If your examples lead you to conclude that Russia has several kinds of economy existing side by side, that's okay.

4. Pretend you are an author of this textbook. The publisher tells you to expand the explanation of each of the factors of production. Pick any one of the four and give it an expanded explanation, liberally using your own illustrations.

5. Imagine that you have just been named new president of Topps and the board of directors wants you to lead the firm in introducing a new product. Write below your introduction and explanation of the new product.

6. Someone at some time in history must have sincerely believed that communism was the best way to run an economy. Develop a strong defense for this national economic form, at least as a theory.

7. Explain with numerous examples and illustrations the law of demand and the law of supply.

8. Having read about how the U.S. government determines and implements its monetary policies, you are now in a position to explain what the relationship is between the money supply and inflation. Go ahead and do so.

9. Explain for a person who has never heard of them what is meant by monetary policies and fiscal policies. Be sure to stress the differences between the two sets of policies.

DISCUSSION OF BUSINESS CASE 1

Ever since the latter three decades of the previous century, the people of the United States have seemed to be against the existence of monopolies in the private sector. In the early days, a firm that dominated a given industry was called a "trust," and that is why to this day we refer to the antitrust activities of the Department of Justice. Even though in those early days there seems to have been great enthusiasm for curbing the monopolistic tendencies of some of the powerful railroads of that era and of giant firms such as Standard Oil under John D. Rockefeller, the antitrust movement went forward only by halting spurts. Political forces thwarted the movement, especially in the U.S. Senate around the turn of the century. In addition, the courts often nullified whatever Congress came up with as a solution. In this most recent merger of AT&T with McCaw, one is tempted to wonder if the federal government was caught napping. If the Baby Bells already can see creeping monopolistic tendencies in this merger, why can't the government? If it made sense for AT&T to be broken up in 1983 (and some keen observers will not agree that it made sense), then why is the government allowing that communication giant to become monopolistic again? Or can it be that the Baby Bells are making accusations that are invalid? When the competition gets tough in American business, one defensive tactic could be to claim that your competitor is breaking some law--whether such is true or not. The case seems to illustrate beautifully that if the people of a nation desire to eliminate monopolies, especially in the private sector, that elimination will require something more than just a desire. What is needed is a government that is ever vigilant, watching for the appearance just over the horizon of new monopolistic tendencies.

1. Do the Baby Bells have a legitimate basis for claiming that AT&T is going to take business away from them and then have a monopoly as a result of the merger with McCaw? Why or why not?

2. Comment on this statement that a communications expert might have made: "This squabble between the Baby Bells and AT&T has nothing to do with today. What is involved here is how the communications industry will be configured fifteen years from now."

3. When it comes to the providing of long-distance telephone service in the United States market today, explain which degree of competition exists, and tell why you arrived at your conclusion.

4. Try to relate the concepts of "productivity" and "growth" to the present confrontation between AT&T-McCaw and the Baby Bells.

ANSWERS TO TRUE-FALSE QUESTIONS

1.	F (p. 6)			6.	T	(p. 10)
2.	T (p. 6)			7.	F	(p. 11)
3.	F (p. 6)			8.	F	(p. 14)
4.	F (p. 8-9)			9.	F	(p. 15)
5.	F (p. 8)			10.	T	(p. 18)

ANSWERS TO MULTIPLE CHOICE QUESTIONS

1.	a (p. 16)	11.	d (p. 11)
2.	c (p. 18-9)	12.	c (p. 11)
3.	d (p. 21)	13.	b (p. 11)
4.	a (p. 6-7)	14.	c (p. 13)
5.	c (p. 6)	15.	a (p. 13)
6.	d (p. 7)	16.	a (p. 15)
7.	b (p. 8-9)	17.	b (p. 14)
8.	d (p. 8)	18.	d (p. 15)
9.	b (p. 10)	19.	c (p. 16)
10.	a (p. 10)	20.	a (p. 19)

CHAPTER TWO

SETTING UP BUSINESS IN THE UNITED STATES

CHAPTER OVERVIEW

A look at the history of U.S. business shows a steady development from sole proprietorships to today's intricate corporate structures. That history has seen us move through: the colonial period; the factory system and the Industrial Revolution; the entrepreneurial era; the production era; the marketing era; and the global era. All businesses fall into one of three categories: sole proprietorship; partnership; or corporation. When forming a corporation, factors to be considered and understood are: stock ownership; stockholders' rights; and the role of the board of directors. Preferred stock guarantees holders fixed dividends but no voting rights. Common stock usually pays dividends only if the corporation makes a profit but it has voting rights. In recent years, special issues have arisen in the corporate world: mergers and acquisitions; multinational corporations; joint ventures; and ownership by employees (through the ESOP--employee stock ownership plan) and by institutions. There are almost ten thousand ESOPs in the United States today. Institutional investors, such as mutual funds and pension funds, because they control enormous resources, can buy very large blocks of stock.

LEARNING OBJECTIVES

1. Trace the history of business in the United States.

2. Identify the major forms of business ownership.

3. Describe sole proprietorships and partnerships and explain the advantages and disadvantages of each.

4. Describe corporations and explain their advantages and disadvantages.

5. Describe the basic issues involved in creating and managing a corporation.

6. Identify recent trends and issues in corporate ownership.

DISCUSSION OF THE OPENING VIGNETTE

The Walden Paddlers organization of alliances makes good sense. So good, in fact, that it is easy to forget what the historically "normal" way has been to start such an operation. One acceptable "traditional" manner would have been to erect a large manufacturing facility, fill it with design engineers, eager kayak-assembly workers, and an administrative staff. Then, a sales network would be necessary, not to mention a trucking fleet to deliver the product to retail outlets contacted by the sales force. To make the new Walden Paddlers "family" feel warm and secure, it would be necessary to pay respectable wages and provide for all the fringe benefits--including expensive medical coverage. All of this would take place before one boat had been sold. This would mean that a lot of expense was being incurred by the firm before a penny of revenue was arriving at the cash drawer. All of this cumbersome organization is often referred to as "overhead." In seasons of the year when kayaks would not be selling in retail stores, the firm would still maintain its large staff, hoping to keep them busy at something. More and more, it is being discovered in all areas of business that there are great economies to be realized in maintaining a small nucleus of a staff and that rush periods can be handled by calling for "temps" (temporary workers) when the existing workforce cannot handle everything. The faculty at the college or university that you attend could be a part of this same plan. Rather than keeping a large group of full-time professors on board (regardless of the number of students enrolled), it is possible to follow the Walden example. And this translates into adding some part-time instructors (to a small regular faculty) if and when additional student enrollment warrants such a move.

1. If the demand for Walden Paddlers' kayaks expands by fifty times some spring, will the current arrangement be able to expand rapidly enough to meet the demand? Why or why not?

2. Looking at Paul Farrow's operation, explain why you consider or do NOT consider him a manager in the traditional sense.

3. Of the terms listed below, pick the one that you think best and most completely describes Paul Farrow's role with Walden Paddlers. Here are your choices: manager, coordinator, chairman of the board, entrepreneur, partner, circus ringmaster, innovator, or orchestra conductor.

4. A young job applicant who has just talked to Paul Farrow about a job tells you the following story. "I told him that I had a spectacular design for a faster and less expensive kayak. He told me that he was not the man to talk to about it. I don't get it." Explain to the applicant what is going on.

ANNOTATED KEY TERMS

<u>Industrial Revolution</u> - A major change in production in the mid-eighteenth century characterized by a shift to the factory system, mass production, and the specialization of labor.

<u>Production era</u> - The period during the early twentieth century in which U.S. business focused almost primarily on improving productivity and manufacturing efficiency.

<u>Marketing concept</u> - The philosophy that to be profitable a business must focus on identifying and satisfying consumer wants.

<u>Sole proprietorship</u> - A business owned and usually operated by one person who is responsible for all its debts.

<u>Unlimited liability</u> - The legal principle holding owners responsible for paying off all the debts of a business.

<u>General partnership</u> - A business with two or more owners who share in both the operation of the firm and the financial responsibility for its debts.

<u>Limited liability</u> - The legal principle holding investors liable for a firm's debts only to the limits of their personal investments in it.

<u>Corporation</u> - A business that is legally considered an entity separate from its owners and that is liable for its own debts; the owners' liability extends to the limits of their investments.

<u>Public corporation</u> - A corporation whose stock is widely held and available for sale to the general public.

<u>Private corporation</u> - A corporation whose stock is held by only a few people and is not available for sale to the general public.

<u>Double taxation</u> - The situation in which taxes may be payable both by a corporation on its profits and by shareholders on dividend incomes.

<u>Corporate governance</u> - The role of shareholders, directors, and other managers in corporate decision making.

<u>Articles of incorporation</u> - A document detailing the corporate governance of a company, including its name and address, its purpose, and the amount of stock it intends to issue.

<u>Corporate bylaws</u> - A document detailing corporate rules and regulations, including the election and responsibilities of directors and procedures for issuing new stock.

<u>Stock</u> - A share of ownership in a corporation.

<u>Stockholder</u> <u>or</u> <u>shareholder</u> - An owner of shares of stock in a corporation.

<u>Dividends</u> - Business profits distributed to shareholders on a per-share basis.

<u>Preferred stock</u> - Stock that guarantees its owners fixed dividends and priority claims over assets but no corporate voting rights.

<u>Common stock</u> - Stock that guarantees voting rights but has the last claims over assets.

<u>Proxy</u> - Authorization granted by a shareholder for someone else to vote his or her shares.

<u>Board of directors</u> - The governing body of a corporation, which reports to its shareholders and delegates power to run its day-to-day operations.

<u>Chief executive officer</u> - The top manager hired by the board of directors to run a corporation.

<u>Inside directors</u> - Directors who, as its top managers, have primary responsibility for a corporation.

<u>Outside directors</u> - Directors who are not employees of a corporation in the normal sense of business.

<u>Merger</u> - The union of two corporations to form a new corporation.

<u>Acquisition</u> - The purchase of one company by another.

<u>Multinational corporation</u> - A corporation that conducts operations and marketing activities on an international scale.

<u>Joint venture (or strategic alliance)</u> - Collaboration between two or more organizations on an enterprise.

<u>Employee stock ownership plan (ESOP)</u> - An arrangement in which a corporation holds its own stock in trust for its employees, who gradually receive ownership of the stock and control of its voting rights.

<u>Institutional investors</u> - Large investors, such as mutual funds and pension funds, that purchase large blocks of corporate stock.

TRUE-FALSE QUESTIONS

1. The English colonists who arrived in North America in the seventeenth century had two choices: farm or starve.

2. With the coming of the Industrial Revolution, mass production allowed firms to purchase raw materials at better prices by buying in large lots.

3. The growth of corporations and improved assembly-line output came at the expense of worker freedom.

4. Scientific management was the first system aimed at increasing worker satisfaction and morale on the job.

5. Although owned by a single individual, the individual does not assume unlimited liability for the sole proprietorship.

6. Freedom is perhaps the most important benefit of sole proprietorships.

7. In an acquisition, one corporation buys another outright.

8. Holders of preferred stock will normally have voting rights.

9. Corporate alliances offer the advantage of allowing each firm to remain independent while sharing the risk of a new venture with another firm.

10. There is a legal limit to the number of partners that may be involved in forming a general partnership.

MULTIPLE CHOICE QUESTIONS

1. During which period did mass production reduce duplication of equipment and allow firms to purchase raw materials at better prices?

    a. colonial period
    b. Industrial Revolution
    c. entrepreneurial era
    d. the production era

2. Who is generally considered by historians to have been the founder of U. S. Steel?

    a. Andrew Carnegie
    b. Andrew Mellon
    c. John D. Rockefeller
    d. J.P. Morgan

3. Scientific management was given further impetus when, in 1913, he introduced the moving assembly line and ushered in the production era. Who was he?

    a. Henry Ford
    b. Andrew Carnegie
    c. Eli Whitney
    d. Cyrus McCormick

4. It is looked upon as the very first legal form of business organization. Which is it?

    a. general partnership
    b. corporation
    c. limited partnership
    d. sole proprietorship

5. Which of the following is a disadvantage of the sole proprietorship?

    a. limited liability
    b. preferred stock
    c. lack of continuity
    d. freedom

6. Which of the following is a disadvantage of the general partnership?

    a. limit to the number of partners
    b. unlimited liability
    c. ability to grow
    d. most difficult business organization to form

7. Select from the list below that which Chief Justice Marshall was referring to when he said in 1819, "an artificial being, invisible, intangible, and existing only in contemplation of the law."

    a. corporation
    b. taxation
    c. copyright
    d. ownership

8. According to the textbook, which of the following is the biggest advantage of the corporation?

    a. funds easily acquired
    b. limited liability
    c. public support
    d. identification

9. In the "double taxation" endured by corporations, which of the following is the second taxation?

    a. property tax on owners
    b. tax on corporate profits
    c. tax on dividends
    d. value-added tax

10. Corporate governance includes three distinct bodies. Which of the following is not one of those bodies, according to the textbook?

    a. stockholders
    b. board of directors
    c. corporate officers
    d. major contract suppliers

11. Which of the following is NOT usually a characteristic of preferred stock?

    a. fixed dividend
    b. voting rights
    c. priority over common on dividends
    d. priority over common on assets

12. They are defined as "typically attorneys, accountants, university officials, and executives from other firms." Who are they?

    a. auditors
    b. corporate managers
    c. outside directors
    d. foremen

13. When one corporation buys another corporation outright, we generally call this action--

    a. institutional ownership
    b. merger
    c. acquisition
    d. hostile takeover

14. Select from the list below a term that means the same thing as "strategic alliance."

    a. multinational corporation
    b. joint venture
    c. insured operation
    d. part of military-industrial complex

15. They are "essentially trusts established on behalf of the employees" of a corporation. They are better known as--

    a. bonded investments
    b. pay raises
    c. child care at the workplace
    d. ESOPs

16. The national teachers retirement system TIAA-CREF has assets of over $95 billion and invests over one-third of that amount in stocks. We would refer to TIAA-CREF as--

    a. semi-affluent
    b. price setter in the bond market
    c. an ESOP
    d. institutional investor

17. English colonists who arrived in North America in the seventeenth century had two choices. One choice was to farm. The other choice was to--

    a. seek work in town
    b. starve
    c. open trading posts with the Indians
    d. hunt

18. According to the marketing concept, business starts with--

    a. the customer
    b. human resources
    c. raw material
    d. funding

19. It is the principle that the government should not interfere in the economy but should instead let business function without regulation according to its own "natural" laws. This principle is called--

    a. natural selection
    b. entrepreneurship
    c. laissez-faire
    d. invisible hand

20. According to the theorists who supported it, "scientific management" did which of the following?

    a. increased employees' sense of well-being
    b. cut down inventory stockpiles
    c. increased efficiency
    d. combined scientific discoveries with manager training

WRITING TO LEARN

1. Perhaps with the help of a textbook in American history, completely explain the atmosphere of business in one of the historical periods treated in this chapter.

2. Using at least one outside reference source, develop a narrative that describes the effect of scientific management on job performance. Then, treat the effect it had on the morale of workers.

3. Being sure to include the contributions of as many factors and persons as possible, compose a sketch of the development of assembly line production as we know it today.

4. Explain why and how the American economy started expanding so swiftly right after the end of World War II. What part did the "marketing concept" play in these good economic times?

5. Choose one of the three--sole proprietorship, partnership, or corporation. Then explain as completely as possible both the advantages and disadvantages of the form of business organization you have chosen.

6. Using several illustrations that you have made up specifically for this essay, explain what is meant by "double taxation" of the corporation.

7. The matter of liability--whether limited or unlimited--is a major concern for business owners. Assume that Arthur Smith's firm is being sued for $1 million more than its insurance covers. Explain the differing impacts of such a lawsuit on: (a) Arthur Smith the <u>sole proprietor</u>, and (b) the Arthur Smith <u>Corporation</u>.

8. Who actually runs a large corporation: top managers, board of directors, executive committee, inside directors, outside directors, creditors, stockholders, or workers with ESOPs? Don't feel bad if you can't answer; even the experts often disagree on this matter of corporate governance. Nevertheless, make an attempt to explain where the ultimate decisions are made in a corporation.

9. Let's assume that you have been named chairman of the board of directors of a big city newspaper that also owns a major TV station in that same market. All members of the previous board of directors have resigned because the newspaper and TV station have been losing money. You are to form a board of twenty members that will be charged with getting the operation back into profit. Explain whom you will place on that board and why.

DISCUSSION OF BUSINESS CASE 2

Apparently, James D. Robinson III held tremendous power in his hands at American Express. Note that he was chief executive officer (CEO) as well as chairman of the board of directors. If, as CEO, he committed a blunder, then he deserved to be reprimanded by the board chairman. But the board chairman was himself. That arrangement works well for the person with the two titles so long as the board of directors is made up of individuals who consider board service an honor and a way to while away some leisure time. Such a board is referred to as a "rubber stamp"; whatever the CEO wants to do, they approve it. In relatively recent times, however, board members for all sorts of organizations--business as well as not-for-profit--have learned the hard way that they bear certain responsibilities. And when a company starts to fail, it is the board's duty to take action. That is very difficult if the board is made up of people who know nothing about the business of the firm. For example, a massive banking corporation may wish to honor a war-hero general, a movie actress, and a great novelist. They do so by placing these personages on their board. It's a good public relations move. But when highly-intricate financial issues come before the board and crucial, life-saving decisions must be made, can we be sure that these "stars" know enough about finance and banking to vote intelligently? Deciding that a CEO is performing poorly is difficult, because very often a board of directors is made up of friends of the CEO--persons that the CEO has invited on the board in the first place. So, while all the CEO's friends are thinking about what is best for the CEO and for his or her career, who, pray tell, is thinking about what is best for the corporation? In the American Express case, enough business-qualified members of the board became greatly concerned over the health of the corporation. Personal concern for Mr. Robinson was, for them, a lower priority.

1. Do you feel that a CEO should have a hand in selecting members of his or her firm's board of directors? Why or why not.

2. Express your opinion concerning the advisability of assembling a "rubber stamp" board of directors. Why do such boards still exist?

3. Should members of a corporate board of directors be paid? How does their pay status affect the burden of responsibility that will fall upon the board?

4. React to this statement that could have been made by a board member at American Express after the CEO's report: "I see some negative aspects to the picture, but the CEO is being paid handsomely to stay on top of things and I know that he will. I'm not worried about it."

ANSWERS TO TRUE-FALSE QUESTIONS

1.	T (p. 27)		6.	T	(p. 31)
2.	T (p. 28)		7.	T	(p. 39)
3.	T (p. 29)		8.	F	(p. 38)
4.	F (p. 28-9)		9.	T	(p. 39-40)
5.	F (p. 31)		10.	F	(p. 32)

ANSWERS TO MULTIPLE CHOICE QUESTIONS

1.	b (p. 28)		11.	b	(p. 38)
2.	a (p. 28)		12.	c	(p. 39)
3.	a (p. 29)		13.	c	(p. 39)
4.	d (p. 31)		14.	b	(p. 40-41)
5.	c (p. 32)		15.	d	(p. 42)
6.	b (p. 32-33)		16.	d	(p. 44)
7.	a (p. 35)		17.	b	(p. 27)
8.	b (p. 35)		18.	a	(p. 30)
9.	c (p. 36)		19.	c	(p. 28)
10.	d (p. 38)		20.	c	(p. 28)

CHAPTER THREE

CONDUCTING BUSINESS ETHICALLY AND RESPONSIBLY

CHAPTER OVERVIEW

Ethics are beliefs about what is right and wrong or good and bad in actions that affect others. Besides situational factors, differences in individual ethical codes can be attributed to family, peers, and personal experiences. Within the workplace, the company itself becomes an additional factor in influencing ethical behavior. Social responsibility refers to the way in which a business behaves toward other groups and individuals in its social environment--customers, other businesses, employees and investors. In defining its sense of social responsibility, a firm typically confronts, in addition, its responsibility toward the environment and is concerned with air, water, and land pollution. In 1980, Congress created the so-called Superfund to help clean up heavily polluted land; the EPA administers the program. Consumerism is social activism dedicated to protecting the rights of consumers in their dealings with businesses. Whistle-blowers are employees who detect and try to put an end to a company's unethical, illegal, and/or socially irresponsible actions by publicizing them. Insider trading occurs when someone uses confidential information to gain from the purchase or sale of stocks. The three most common approaches to social responsibility are: social obligation, social reaction, and social response.

LEARNING OBJECTIVES

1. Explain how individuals develop personal codes of ethics and why ethics are important in the workplace.

2. Distinguish social responsibility from ethics and trace the evolution of social responsibility in U.S. business.

3. Show how the concept of social responsibility applies to environmental issues and to a firm's relationships with customers, employees, and investors.

4. Identify three general approaches to social responsibility and describe the four steps that a firm must take to implement a social responsibility program.

5. Explain how issues of social responsibility and ethics affect small businesses.

DISCUSSION OF THE OPENING VIGNETTE

Notice this key closing line from the opening vignette: "Consumers were convinced that Pepsi had treated them honestly and openly throughout the crisis and that the public welfare had always been the company's first concern." To achieve that degree of public confidence was very difficult for Pepsi during the tampering scare. Currently, the tobacco industry is under some scrutiny by Congress. Without taking sides in that dispute, merely ask yourself: Can the following be said of a tobacco firm? "The public welfare had always been the company's first concern." Answer that question as you wish. Returning now to Pepsi, from an ethical standpoint, there is a differentiation that must be established. On the one hand, there is the matter of a firm actually being genuinely concerned about the public welfare. In contrast, there is the matter of appearing to the public as if the firm is genuinely concerned. The latter approach is merely a public relations gig. Many a large firm with a talented propaganda staff can pull off this trick time after time. But somewhere down the line, the firm's true self will show through. The vignette cites Johnson and Johnson's handling of the Tylenol scare. Many previous writers on that case seem to agree that Johnson and Johnson took the approach: We have to do what is right regardless of what it will cost us! To make things more complicated, successful handling of such panics is not an "either-or" situation with a choice between genuine concern and publicity gimmickry. Rather, the genuine concern must be accompanied with public relations efforts to alert the public to just what the firm is doing to handle the problem. Pepsi used this two-pronged approach. It cannot be denied that very helpful to their cause was having FDA Commissioner David Kessler helping them in their damage control campaign. One can guess, however, that Mr. Kessler would not have been so helpful if he thought that Pepsi was running a first-class cover-up.

1. Comment upon this statement: "Whether your firm cares or doesn't care about the public welfare is not important. What really matters is that the public thinks you care about them."

2. The vignette referred to a "crisis management team." Assume you are a Pepsi executive and you have been asked to form such a team. List the various areas of the company from which you would select members of this team and explain each of your choices.

3. List the three major tasks, as you see them, for that crisis management team or for any other group charged with a similar mission.

4. The Pepsi crisis has passed, and you, as the Pepsi CEO, wish to distribute a one-sentence statement on how Pepsi will handle such cases in the future. Please write that sentence.

ANNOTATED KEY TERMS

Ethics - Beliefs about what is right and wrong or good and bad in actions that affect others.

Ethical behavior - Behavior conforming to generally accepted social norms concerning beneficial and harmful actions.

Social responsibility - The attempt of a business to balance its commitments to groups and individuals in its environment, including customers, other businesses, employees, and investors.

Superfund - Special fund set up by Congress and administered by the EPA to help clean up heavily polluted land.

Environmental Protection Agency (EPA) - Federal agency established to protect and encourage the conservation of natural resources.

Consumerism - Form of social activism dedicated to protecting the rights of consumers in their dealings with businesses.

Collusion - Illegal agreement between two or more companies to commit a wrongful act.

Whistle-blower - Employee who detects and tries to put an end to a company's unethical, illegal, or socially irresponsible actions by publicizing them.

Check kiting - Illegal practice of writing checks against money that has not yet been credited at the bank on which they are drawn.

Insider trading - Use of information unavailable to the general public to profit from stock transactions.

Social-obligation approach - Approach to social responsibility by which a company meets only minimum legal requirements in its commitments to groups and individuals in its social environment.

Social-reaction approach - Approach to social responsibility by which a company, if specifically asked to do so, exceeds legal minimums in its commitments to groups and individuals in its social environment.

Social-response approach - Approach to social responsibility by which a company actively seeks opportunities to contribute to the well-being of groups and individuals in its social environment.

Social audit - Systematic analysis of a firm's success in using funds earmarked for meeting its social responsibility goals.

TRUE-FALSE QUESTIONS

1. Although family and personal experiences tend to shape a person's individual code of ethics, it is generally agreed that a person's peers have no such effect.

2. To demonstrate commitment to ethical practices, many companies have adopted codes of ethics that formally acknowledge their intent to do business in an ethical manner.

3. Although ethics is important, up to now no major corporation has gone so far as to produce a written code of ethics.

4. In the area of social responsibility, a firm owes it to its customers to maximize the profits of the firm.

5. As a rule, toxic waste can be neither destroyed nor processed into harmless material.

6. Unethical and irresponsible business practices toward customers can result in government fines and penalties.

7. Consumerism is social activism dedicated to protecting the rights of consumers in their dealings with businesses.

8. As a rule, according to the textbook's definition, whistle-blowers combat unethical practices within their firms but do not spread knowledge of such practices to sources outside the firm.

9. Check kiting is basically nothing more than writing a check for a very large amount.

10. The "most liberal" approach to social responsibility is the social-response approach.

MULTIPLE CHOICE QUESTIONS

1. Which of the following is NOT mentioned by the textbook as an influence on a person's individual code of ethics?

    a. involvement in team sports
    b. family
    c. personal experiences
    d. interactions with company and peers

2. In influencing ethical behavior within a company, which of the following does the textbook identify as "perhaps the single most effective step" in that process?

    a. establish written codes of ethical conduct
    b. conduct and develop clear ethical positions
    c. thoroughly brief new employees
    d. demonstrate the commitment of top management

3. It is defined as the way a business behaves toward other groups and individuals in its social environment. What is it?

    a. efficiency
    b. basic fundamental goodness
    c. social responsibility
    d. social awareness

4. Which of the following is NOT mentioned by the textbook as those other groups and individuals with which a firm interacts in a social setting?

    a. customers
    b. other businesses
    c. employees
    d. government

5. What is the specific term that we use to describe what occurs when sulfur is pumped into the atmosphere, mixes with natural moisture, and then falls as precipitation?

    a. air pollution
    b. acid rain
    c. sulfur dust
    d. lead precipitate

6. Because of pollution by an Eastman Kodak plant, it was literally possible to--

    a. start a fire in the river
    b. find ashes in the dust bin
    c. develop photographs in the river water
    d. make a grenade from toxic waste

7. What is defined as dangerous chemical and/or radioactive byproducts of manufacturing processes?

    a. toxic wastes
    b. hazardous residue
    c. non-treated slurge
    d. recycled contaminants

8. Which of the following is NOT a characteristic of the EPA Superfund arrangement?

   a. some of its funds have been spent to locate problems
   b. chemical and oil companies pay a special tax
   c. little of its funds have been spent on actual cleanup
   d. instituted by Congress in 1989

9. Which one of the following is the best example of a firm exercising social responsibility toward the environment?

   a. Eastman Kodak
   b. Champion International Corporation
   c. Elf Atochem
   d. Herman Miller, Inc.

10. When Procter & Gamble ran afoul of the FDA over Citrus Hill Fresh Choice, how was the problem eliminated?

   a. change in manufacturing process
   b. change in labeling
   c. discontinuing the product
   d. stopping hazardous dumping

11. Which of the following is NOT one of the four basic consumer rights proposed by President John F. Kennedy?

   a. right to safe products
   b. right of consumers to choose what they buy
   c. right to lowest possible prices
   d. right to be heard

12. When firms that are supposed to be competing with one another agree to collaborate on such wrongful acts as price fixing, we call this practice--

   a. price gouging
   b. bait and switch
   c. adulteration
   d. collusion

13. When the firm switched from individual wrapping to bottles, prices went up tremendously. Name the firm.

   a. Wal-Mart
   b. Du Pont Merck
   c. Elf Atochem
   d. C. R. Bard

14. What do we call employees who detect and try to put an end to a company's unethical, illegal, and/or socially irresponsible actions by publicizing them?

    a. corporate spies
    b. ethicists
    c. whistle-blowers
    d. pragmatists

15. Ivan Boesky, Dennis Levine, and the firm of Drexel Burnham Lambert. All are part of a textbook illustration of--

    a. insider trading
    b. check kiting
    c. stock pools
    d. poor financial management

16. Of the four choices below, one is NOT an approach to social responsibility listed by the textbook. Identify the item that is out of place.

    a. social-obligation approach
    b. social-reaction approach
    c. social-duty approach
    d. social-response approach

17. Which of the following is looked upon as the "most liberal" approach to social responsibility?

    a. social-obligation approach
    b. social-reaction approach
    c. social-duty approach
    d. social-response approach

18. Which of the following firms is known to earmark 2.4 percent of pretax earnings for worthy projects?

    a. Eastman Kodak
    b. Levi Strauss
    c. Texaco
    d. Elf Atochem

19. It is a systematic analysis of a firm's success in using funds that it has earmarked for its social responsibility goals. What is it called?

    a. social audit
    b. responsibility analysis
    c. waste barrier
    d. management by charity

20. How has South Shore Bank in Chicago shown its sense of social responsibility?

    a.   sponsorship of soup kitchens for the poor
    b.   establishing an entire league of softball teams
    c.   helping to rebuild a declining neighborhood
    d.   paying high interest on savings accounts

WRITING TO LEARN

1. Explain why a firm's code of ethical behavior should or should not make references to the matters of sexual discrimination and/or sexual harassment?

2. No doubt about it, whistle-blowers often bring themselves lots of grief. Tell why you think this is so.

3. Let us say that you always buy the products of a particular nationally-known manufacturer. When you hear that this favorite firm of yours has openly and profusely polluted a nearby stream, will this make you change your mind about buying their products? Would the fact that the firm has now stopped this pollution affect your answer? How?

4. Evaluate this statement: "If you think that ethical lessons can be learned from peers, then you are making a major mistake."

5. Write a mini-essay on why you would or would NOT ask a prospective employer (in an interview) just which steps his or her firm has taken to assure ethical conduct.

6. Is there any truth at all to this statement? "The last thing on the mind of a business person is ethical conduct. Making a profit comes before everything." Explain why you answered as you did.

7. The textbook indicates that a firm has a social responsibility to its investors. Tell what this means and why you think this is so.

8. If you believe in recycling, tell why you feel it is necessary. If you do NOT believe in recycling, tell why all the emphasis on it is foolish. If you take the second approach, then please offer an effective alternative to recycling.

9. Take any one of the four basic consumer rights proposed by President John F. Kennedy and give it a full explanation, incorporating several examples as illustrations.

DISCUSSION OF BUSINESS CASE 3

The Lopez case provides a perfect illustration of why unethical conduct takes place: the pressures can become severe. The case hints that neither General Motors nor Volkswagen has a totally spotless record. This might be a good point at which to indicate that <u>firms</u> do not cheat nor do they engage in unethical conduct. Only <u>persons</u> can do that. So, when billions of dollars are at stake, individuals can easily give in to the temptation to forget what they have learned about ethical conduct. The more money involved and the more job jeopardy that may be possible for an executive, the greater the tendency for that executive to try something underhanded. Also, one social responsibility can be fighting against another. Here's how. According to the textbook, a firm has an obligation to other businesses. This obligation would dictate fair play. However, a firm also has an obligation to its investors--to make and distribute a profit. If unethical conduct can prevent that profit picture from suffering, then the firm committing unethical acts has done something to enrich the lives of their investors. The case also makes us aware that eternal vigilance is necessary. This means keeping constant watch on your firm's employees to be sure that they are not improvising around the firm's ethical code. How does a top executive prevent unethical conduct in his or her firm? The text suggests that the secret is to be sure that the CEO commands adherence by all employees to the firm's code of ethics. Said another way, the CEO must not be a hypocrite. That is, if even one employee senses that the CEO <u>talks</u> good ethics but <u>acts</u> in such a way that profit comes before ethics, then the CEO's words are meaningless. To a lesser degree, eternal vigilance can also mean keeping an eye on what employees of your competitors are doing. But theory on the subject teaches that unethical conduct by competitors is no excuse for your own unethical conduct.

1. There's an old saying: "Avoid the appearance of evil." Do you think that Volkswagen has avoided the appearance of evil?

2. Discuss the merits of the VW top executive saying to Mr. Lopez: "Sorry, but the way this affair has mushroomed out of proportion, we just cannot take you on our staff. The public fallout will be too great."

3. Is the following "commandment" too demanding? "If the only way to succeed in your industry is to engage in the regular cheating that is going on right now, then get out of that industry!"

4. What can General Motors do now to restore its reputation for honesty and ethical behavior in the eyes of its suppliers?

ANSWERS TO TRUE-FALSE QUESTIONS

1.	F (p. 51)	6.	T (p. 58)
2.	T (p. 52)	7.	T (p. 58)
3.	F (p. 52)	8.	F (p. 59)
4.	F (p. 52)	9.	F (p. 60)
5.	T (p. 56)	10.	T (p. 64)

ANSWERS TO MULTIPLE CHOICE QUESTIONS

1.	a (p. 51)	11.	c (p. 59)
2.	d (p. 51)	12.	d (p. 59)
3.	c (p. 52)	13.	b (p. 59)
4.	d (p. 52)	14.	c (p. 59)
5.	b (p. 55)	15.	a (p. 60)
6.	c (p. 56)	16.	c (p. 63)
7.	a (p. 56)	17.	d (p. 64)
8.	d (p. 57)	18.	b (p. 64)
9.	d (p. 57)	19.	a (p. 64)
10.	b (p. 58)	20.	c (p. 53)

CHAPTER FOUR

UNDERSTANDING INTERNATIONAL BUSINESS

CHAPTER OVERVIEW

We often take for granted the diversity of goods and services available today as a result of international trade. The world economy is fast becoming a single interdependent system, a process called globalization. An absolute advantage exists when a country can produce something more cheaply than any other country. A country has a comparative advantage in goods that it can make more cheaply or better than other goods. Trading with other nations can pose problems if a country's imports and exports do not strike an acceptable balance. There are two ways to measure this import-export relationship: balance of trade and balance of payments. For years now, U.S. imports have greatly exceeded exports. An exchange rate is the rate at which the currency of one nation can be exchanged for that of another. There are several levels of international involvement for a firm: exporter-importer; international firm; or multinational firm. Some international organizational strategies are: independent agents; licensing arrangements; branch offices; strategic alliances; direct investment; and global business. Barriers to international trade can be: social-cultural; economic; or legal-political. Examples of the latter type of barrier would be tariffs and quotas. GATT seeks to reduce or eliminate trade barriers such as tariffs and quotas.

LEARNING OBJECTIVES

1. Identify the major world marketplaces and explain how different forms of competitive advantage, import-export balances, exchange rates, and foreign competition determine the ways in which countries and businesses respond to the international environment.

2. Discuss the factors involved in deciding to do business internationally and in selecting the appropriate levels of international involvement and international organizational structure.

3. Describe some of the ways in which social, cultural, economic, legal, and political differences among nations affect international business and explain how trade agreements assist world trade.

DISCUSSION OF THE OPENING VIGNETTE

Certainly, no one can criticize Ford for wanting to produce a product that would be accepted by car buyers all over the world with only the most minor of modifications being required. Millions and billions of dollars could be saved if one basic product would satisfy the world. Ford is to be commended for its efforts, and there are splendid possibilities that the "world car" idea will be a success. However, we cannot help but note that there is an irony in here. Some years ago, Ford was praised by international business chapters in textbooks as the American automaker that had been most adaptive in marketing its product in Europe. While most U.S. automotive firms were making and selling large, bulky American cars to Europeans and thus encountering mixed success, Ford was listening to drivers on the continent and then creating cars that satisfied European wants. Ford was also credited with bringing numerous Europeans into its European management structure. When Ford's car-building decisions were being made for Europe, those decisions reflected the wants and desires of the European market. Prior to that time, the U.S. auto industry still turned a relatively deaf ear to consumer demands in Europe--and in Japan. The most glaring example of this was seen in the ignoring of the fact that Japanese and British drivers move forward on the <u>left</u> side of a road! This means that drivers in those two nations use cars with the steering wheel on the right side of the front seat. Yet, American car companies continued to market cars in these two countries with the steering wheel on the <u>left</u> side, American style. Yes, producing the "world car" <u>can</u> lead to saving millions and billions, but could such an approach also lead to millions and billions in <u>lost sales</u> because the world car is not a close enough match with foreign demands? Certainly, Ford will be keeping an eye on the situation and will be very serious about making the right decisions.

1. Evaluate this statement that could be made by an American manufacturer: "We make a good product here in the U.S. and we just have to teach those Europeans to appreciate what we make."

2. Whether you have been to Europe or not, give some reasons why American car makers some years ago realized that the typical American car might not sell well in Europe.

3. Based on what you have read in this opening vignette, do you think that a McDonald's in China offers customers the very same menu as a McDonald's in Chicago? Why or why not?

4. If you were chairman of the board at Ford, and a decision had to be made on the "world car," how would you vote?-- (a) one model for all world markets, or (b) a car adapted for each of the major world markets. Explain your decision.

ANNOTATED KEY TERMS

<u>Import</u> - A product made or grown abroad but sold domestically.

<u>Export</u> - A product made or grown domestically but shipped and sold abroad.

<u>Globalization</u> - The process by which the world economy is becoming a single interdependent system.

<u>Absolute advantage</u> - A nation's ability to produce something more cheaply than any other country.

<u>Comparative advantage</u> - A nation's ability to produce some products more cheaply or better than other products.

<u>Balance of trade</u> - Total economic value of all products imported into a country minus the total economic value of all products exported out of it.

<u>Trade deficit</u> - The situation in which a country's imports exceed its exports, creating a negative balance of trade.

<u>Trade surplus</u> - The situation in which a country's exports exceed its imports, creating a positive balance of trade.

<u>Balance of payments</u> - The flow of all money into or out of the country.

<u>Exchange rate</u> - The rate at which the currency of one nation can be exchanged for that of another.

<u>Exporter</u> - A firm that distributes and sells products to one or more foreign countries.

<u>Importer</u> - A firm that buys products in foreign markets and then imports them for resale in its home country.

<u>International firm</u> - A firm that conducts a significant portion of its business in foreign countries.

<u>Multinational firm</u> - A firm that designs, produces, and markets products in many nations.

<u>Independent agent</u> - A foreign individual or organization who agrees to represent an exporter's interests.

<u>Licensing arrangement</u> - An arrangement in which firms choose foreign individuals or organizations to manufacture or market the firm's products in another country.

<u>Royalty</u> - A payment made to a license granter from a licensee in return for the rights to market the licenser's product.

Branch office - A foreign office set up by an international or multinational firm.

Strategic alliance (sometimes called a **joint venture**) - An arrangement in which a company finds a foreign partner to contribute approximately equal amounts of resources and capital to a new business in the partner's country.

Direct investment - An arrangement in which a firm buys or establishes tangible assets in another country.

Countertrading - A form of bartering in which a country requires that a foreign firm buy its products in exchange for the privilege of selling there.

Quota - A restriction on the number of products of a certain type that can be imported into a country.

Embargo - A government order banning exportation and/or importation of a particular product or all the products of a particular country.

Tariff - A tax levied on imported products.

Subsidy - A government payment to help a domestic business compete with foreign firms.

Protectionism - The practice of protecting domestic business at the expense of free-market competition.

Local-content law - A law requiring that products sold in a particular country be at least partly made there.

Cartel - An association of producers whose purpose is to control supply and prices.

Dumping - The practice of selling a product abroad for less than the comparable price charged at home.

General Agreement on Tariffs and Trade (GATT) - An international trade agreement to encourage the multilateral reduction or elimination of trade barriers.

European Community (EC) - An agreement among Western European nations to eliminate internal trade barriers while imposing quotas and tariffs on goods imported from nonmember nations.

North American Free Trade Agreement (NAFTA) - An agreement gradually to eliminate tariffs and other trade barriers between the United States, Canada, and Mexico.

TRUE-FALSE QUESTIONS

1. As more and more firms engage in international business, the world economy is fast becoming a single interdependent system--a process called globalization.

2. The United States dominates the North American business region.

3. No country can produce all the goods and services its people need.

4. Some examples of absolute advantage are: Brazilian timber, Canadian coffee, and Saudi oil.

5. A country has a comparative advantage in goods that it can make more cheaply or better than other goods.

6. The contemporary world economy revolves around three major marketplaces: North America, South America, and Europe.

7. The terms balance of trade and balance of payments mean the same thing.

8. Thanks to an agreement after World War II, fixed exchange rates for currency are the norm today.

9. Companies conducting international operations must watch exchange-rate fluctuations closely because such changes affect overseas demand for their products.

10. For a multinational firm, the location of the firm's headquarters is almost irrelevant.

MULTIPLE CHOICE QUESTIONS

1. The world economy is fast becoming a single interdependent system in a process that is called--

   a. multinationalism
   b. competitive advantage
   c. globalization
   d. importation

2. The contemporary world revolves around three major marketplaces. Which of the following is NOT one of these three major marketplaces?

   a. the China-India complex
   b. North America
   c. Europe
   d. the Pacific Rim

3. One of the following nations is NOT considered to be part of the Pacific Rim. Which is it?

   a. China
   b. Australia
   c. Vietnam
   d. Hong Kong

4. Which of the short statements below best explains the relationship between balance of trade and balance of payments?

   a. balance of trade includes balance of payments
   b. the two terms mean the same thing
   c. balance of payments is rarely figured in dollars
   d. balance of payments includes balance of trade

5. Of the Disney theme parks, which has so far been the biggest disappointment to the Disney organization?

   a. Anaheim, California
   b. Paris, France
   c. Orlando, Florida
   d. Tokyo, Japan

6. Which of the following is NOT given by the textbook as a level of international involvement?

   a. exporter or importer
   b. international firm
   c. multinational firm
   d. regional purveyor

7. Although it may be large and influential in the global economy, it remains basically a domestic firm with international operations. What is it?

   a. an international firm
   b. a multinational firm
   c. a domestic-global organization
   d. GATT

8. The textbook indicates that a major disadvantage of using license holders is--

   a. shipping complications
   b. difficulty in locating effective license holders
   c. the length of time stipulated in most agreements
   d. recurring foreign currency exchange problems

9. A foreign individual or organization who agrees to represent an exporter's interests in foreign markets. What is it?

    a. independent agent
    b. export specialist
    c. balance of payments supervisor
    d. comptroller

10. In international business, the strategic alliance is also referred to as--

    a. licensing
    b. joint venture
    c. franchising
    d. regional adaptation

11. Which American firm has opened a new factory in China to manufacture a vaccine for hepatitis B?

    a. Johnson and Johnson
    b. Monsanto
    c. Dow
    d. Merck

12. Which of the following best describes the facility that Allied-Lyons (as a parent company) has opened in China?

    a. a tire factory
    b. an ice cream parlor
    c. a travel agency
    d. a bank

13. The textbook discusses three major categories of barriers to international trade. These categories are listed below along with an inappropriate item. Identify the inappropriate item.

    a. social-cultural
    b. health conditional
    c. political-legal
    d. economic

14. It restricts the total number of products of a certain type that can be imported into a country. It raises the prices of those imports by reducing their supply. What is it?

    a. tariff
    b. embargo
    c. quota
    d. countertrade

15. They are government payments to help a domestic business compete with foreign firms. They are, in reality, indirect tariffs. What are they called?

   a. quotas
   b. subsidies
   c. revenues
   d. embargoes

16. Many countries, including the United States, have requirements that a foreign product sold in their country must be at least partly made in the country where the product is to be sold. What are such requirements called?

   a. local-content laws
   b. countertrade measures
   c. subsidies
   d. tariffs

17. Let us say that a foreign firm sells one of its products in the United States at a price that is lower than the same firm would sell the product for in its own country. Such a practice is referred to as--

   a. a cartel
   b. franking
   c. allocating
   d. dumping

18. What is the name given to the practice of helping domestic business at the expense of free-market competition by making it more difficult for foreign firms to market their products in our country?

   a. countertrading
   b. subsidizing
   c. protectionism
   d. equalizing

19. Using the terminology of international trade, we can classify OPEC as a--

   a. cartel
   b. trade association
   c. trade agreement
   d. comparative advantage producer

20. Of the business sectors indicated below, which is expected to be the most greatly impacted by the North American Free Trade Agreement (NAFTA)?

   a. services
   b. agriculture
   c. publishing
   d. entertainment

WRITING TO LEARN

1. Assume that you are in charge of opening a series of Burger King restaurants in the area of Berlin, Federal Republic of Germany. What are some adaptations that you feel will be necessary in the menu for the restaurants to be successful in Berlin? Explain each adaptation suggested.

2. After performing some limited research on the subject, explain why the Pacific Rim is expected to be such a significant world market in the years to come.

3. Your firm is entering a new French metropolitan market with a tasty bakery product. Top executives have decided to use American TV commercials (already produced at great expense) and dub in French for use on French TV. You disagree. Explain why the firm should go to the trouble of having a French advertising agency produce new commercials for the French market.

4. Identify the three major world markets and tell as much as you can about each area. Explain why these areas are so important. Explain why other areas of the world are apparently of lesser importance.

5. Using plenty of examples, explain the differences between the concepts of absolute advantage and comparative advantage.

6. Tell why you feel knowing a foreign language would be extremely important for an employee of a firm that plans to branch out into international marketing of its products or services. Or, you may indicate the reasons why you think knowing a foreign language is NOT important.

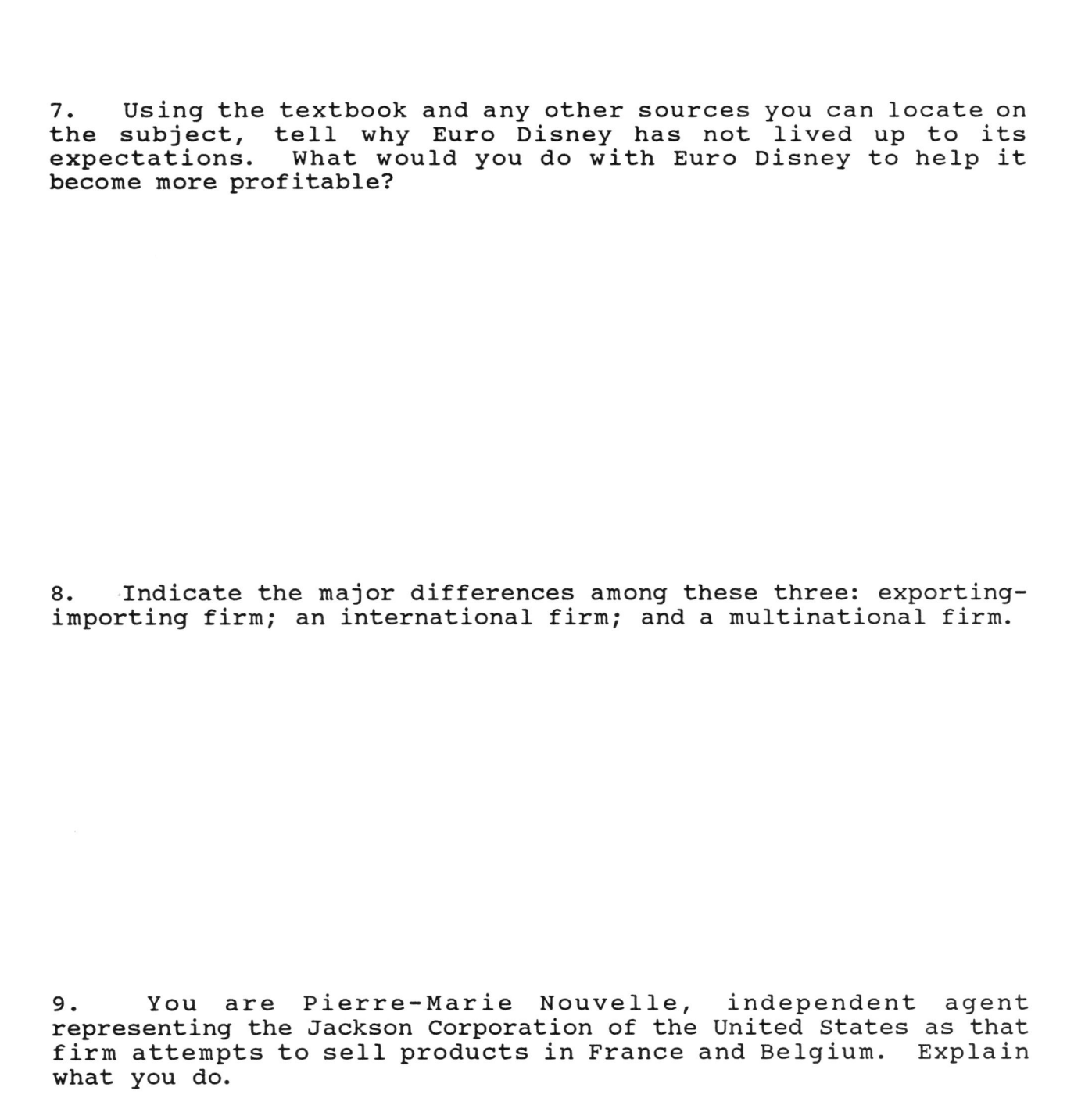

7. Using the textbook and any other sources you can locate on the subject, tell why Euro Disney has not lived up to its expectations. What would you do with Euro Disney to help it become more profitable?

8. Indicate the major differences among these three: exporting-importing firm; an international firm; and a multinational firm.

9. You are Pierre-Marie Nouvelle, independent agent representing the Jackson Corporation of the United States as that firm attempts to sell products in France and Belgium. Explain what you do.

DISCUSSION OF BUSINESS CASE 4

The success of AST Research, Inc. in China is impressive and inspiring. However, so little of the total story is revealed in the Business Case 4 sketch. What can we know of the person-to-person contacts that had to be made for cooperative relationships to be established? In other words, at some point an American representative of AST had to stand face-to-face with an official of the Chinese government or a member of a cooperating Chinese firm. Did AST send an employee who was fluent in the appropriate dialect or was the employee accompanied by a strongly bilingual interpreter? Did the key Chinese and the key American develop a personal friendship? How much difficulty was there in discussing technical matters across the language barrier? Particularly crucial were the talks between the AST representative and the leaders of Beijing Stone. How has AST gone about making contacts in "small businesses, schools, and hospitals" in an effort to sell the idea that computers can be of tremendous help in any form of endeavor? And notice what a large measure of adapting was required: preparing hardware and software that could accommodate Chinese characters instead of letters of the English alphabet. In a very real sense, the first AST personnel who journeyed to China with an idea to sell were like the missionaries of the previous century. One of the most celebrated and chronicled of that era was Dr. David Livingstone. Although many years of his work led to a large contingent of Christians in the heart of deepest Africa, it must have begun by the doctor's arriving in one small village and introducing himself to a few natives. Things tended to go well from there. That first contact was important. The same must have been true with AST. For any firm wishing to follow the example of AST, it is important to understand how the first contacts were set up and just how they were conducted.

1. You are working for a computer firm that wishes to crack the Chinese market and you are getting ready to make a first exploratory journey to China. Who and what will you take with you?

2. Does it appear to you that AST can hold its own once the larger American computer giants come into the China market? Why or why not?

3. Explain why you feel that AST had to make room for the processing of Chinese characters.

4. React to this statement: "Forward-thinking Chinese know that they must adapt to Western ways, and that includes our English alphabet. We aren't helping a Chinese firm one bit if we cater to their obsession with those thousands of characters."

ANSWERS TO TRUE-FALSE QUESTIONS

1. T (p. 72)
2. T (p. 72)
3. T (p. 73)
4. F (p. 73)
5. T (p. 73)
6. F (p. 72)
7. F (p. 73)
8. F (p. 75)
9. T (p. 75)
10. T (p. 79)

ANSWERS TO MULTIPLE CHOICE QUESTIONS

1. c (p. 72)
2. a (p. 72)
3. c (p. 72)
4. d (p. 74-75)
5. b (p. 77)
6. d (p. 78)
7. a (p. 79)
8. c (p. 81)
9. a (p. 80)
10. b (p. 81)
11. d (p. 82)
12. b (p. 82)
13. b (p. 84)
14. c (p. 87-88)
15. b (p. 88)
16. a (p. 89)
17. d (p. 89)
18. c (p. 88)
19. a (p. 89)
20. b (p. 90)

CHAPTER FIVE

MANAGING THE BUSINESS ENTERPRISE

CHAPTER OVERVIEW

The starting point in effective management is setting goals--objectives that a business hopes (and plans) to achieve. Regardless of purpose and mission, every firm needs long-term, intermediate, and short-term goals. Strategy formulation involves three basic steps: setting strategic goals; analyzing the organization and its environment; and matching the organization and its environment. Strategic plans are usually set by the board of directors and top management; tactical plans involve upper and middle management. Contingency planning is planning for change. Crisis management involves an organization's methods for dealing with emergencies. Management is the process of planning, organizing, leading, and controlling. There are three basic levels of management: top; middle; and first-line. Included in the areas of management are: human resources; operations; information; marketing; and finance. Effective managers need to develop technical, human relations, conceptual, and decision-making skills. Corporate culture is defined as the shared experiences, stories, beliefs, and norms that characterize an organization. Corporate culture influences management philosophy, style, and behavior. Corporate culture must be effectively communicated by management to others in the organization.

LEARNING OBJECTIVES

1. Explain the importance of setting goals and formulating strategies as the starting points of effective management.

2. Describe the four activities that constitute the management process.

3. Identify types of managers by level and area.

4. Describe the five basic management skills.

5. Describe the development and explain the importance of corporate culture.

DISCUSSION OF OPENING VIGNETTE

Andy Wilson of Wal-Mart shows us several aspects of the manager's role. Although the narrative doesn't tell us so, we can guess intelligently that at Susanville Andy Wilson became a little stern while indicating to store officials on the scene that he did not like what he saw--"empty shelves, poor displays, department supervisors who cannot answer basic questions, and a few unhappy customers." As the military might express it, someone at Susanville got "chewed out." Despite all that we may read about being a happy manager leading a satisfied workforce, this corrective admonishing is still very much a part of being a manager. In Salem, Oregon, Wilson's role was not to criticize and correct but to inspire a new and already enthusiastic staff. To accomplish this different mission, he resorted to literal cheerleading, passing on to these new employees a bit of the corporate culture of Wal-Mart. Then, when Wilson returned to Bentonville headquarters, he had his staff follow up on the lagging Susanville store. And you can bet that Andy Wilson and his helpers will be keeping an eye on Susanville for a long time. That store had better shape up! Andy Wilson has shown us something else, too. Executives who are willing to work long hours and travel great distances set the example for their subordinates. No one working under Wilson can accuse him of setting a bad example. There is something else to consider here. The narrative tells us that Andy Wilson has responsibility for Wal-Mart stores in seven states. This means he is forced to delegate lots of authority to subordinates--all the way down to the lowest paid employee in the smallest store. To command seven states of Wal-Mart stores, he must keep abreast of the big overall picture, but that doesn't keep him from going down to the "front line" every now and then to see what is really happening. He's like General George S. Patton, Jr. of World War II fame. Patton commanded from the rear but spent many moments right at the front with his troops.

1. Is Andy Wilson wasting valuable time by being out on the road at individual stores when he could be at the home office mapping future strategies? Why or why not?

2. Let your imagination run wild. What do you suppose Andy Wilson said to the store manager and district manager in Susanville to motivate them to get on the ball?

3. Explain why Andy Wilson felt it was necessary to lead that pep rally at the store in Salem, Oregon.

4. Explain what you think the reaction is at a Wal-Mart store when the word is received that "Andy Wilson will be here tomorrow." What about at the Susanville store?

ANNOTATED KEY TERMS

<u>Goals</u> - Objectives that a business hopes and plans to achieve.

<u>Mission statement</u> - The organization's statement of how it will achieve its purpose in the environment in which it conducts its business.

<u>Long-term goals</u> - Goals set for extended periods of time, typically five years or more into the future.

<u>Intermediate goals</u> - Goals set for a period of one to five years into the future.

<u>Short-term goals</u> - Goals set for the very near future, typically less than one year.

<u>Strategy formulation</u> - Creation of a broad program for defining and meeting an organization's goals.

<u>Strategic goals</u> - Long-term goals derived directly from a firm's mission statement.

<u>Environmental analysis</u> - Process of scanning the business environment for threats and opportunities.

<u>Organizational analysis</u> - Process of analyzing a firm's strengths and weaknesses.

<u>Strategic plans</u> - Plans that reflect decisions about resource allocations, company priorities, and steps needed to meet strategic goals.

<u>Tactical plans</u> - Generally short-range plans concerned with implementing specific aspects of a company's strategic plans.

<u>Operational plans</u> - Plans setting short-term targets for daily, weekly, or monthly performance.

<u>Contingency planning</u> - Identifying aspects of a business or its environment that might entail changes in strategy.

<u>Crisis management</u> - An organization's methods for dealing with emergencies.

<u>Management</u> - Process of planning, organizing, leading, and controlling an organization's resources to achieve its goals.

<u>Planning</u> - The management process of determining what an organization needs to do and how best to get it done.

<u>Organizing</u> - The management process of determining the best way to arrange an organization's resources and activities into a coherent structure.

Leading - The management process of guiding and motivating employees to meet an organization's objectives.

Controlling - The management process of monitoring an organization's performance to ensure that it is meeting its goals.

Top managers - Managers responsible to the board of directors and stockholders for a firm's overall performance and effectiveness.

Middle managers - Managers responsible for implementing the strategies, policies, and decisions made by top managers.

First-line managers - Managers responsible for supervising the work of employees.

Human resource managers - Managers responsible for hiring, training, evaluating, and compensating employees.

Operations managers - Managers responsible for production, inventory, and quality control.

Information managers - Managers responsible for designing and implementing systems to gather, organize, and distribute information.

Marketing managers - Managers responsible for getting products from producers to consumers.

Financial managers - Managers responsible for planning and overseeing a firm's accounting functions and financial resources.

Technical skills - The skills needed to perform specialized tasks.

Human relations skills - Skills in understanding and getting along with other people.

Conceptual skills - The abilities to think in the abstract, to diagnose and analyze different situations, and to see beyond the present situation.

Decision-making skills - Skills in defining problems and selecting the best courses of action.

Time-management skills - Skills associated with the productive use of one's time.

Corporate culture - The shared experiences, stories, beliefs, and norms that characterize an organization.

TRUE-FALSE QUESTIONS

1. Goals are defined as objectives that a business hopes (and plans) to achieve.

2. Basically, a mission statement is a description of how a firm is going to carry out a particular task to be finished in a day or two.

3. In this chapter, environmental analysis refers to the careful planning necessary to avoid contaminating the environment around a firm's manufacturing facility.

4. By its very nature, a contingency plan is a hedge against changes that might occur.

5. Management is defined as the process of planning, organizing, leading, and rewarding.

6. In leading, a manager is concerned with guiding and motivating employees to meet the firm's objectives.

7. Titles such as plant manager, operations manager, and division manager designate middle-management slots.

8. As a rule, it is the operations manager that is responsible for getting products from producers to consumers.

9. Technical skills are especially important for top managers.

10. Human relations skills are important at all levels of management.

MULTIPLE CHOICE QUESTIONS

1. They relate to extended periods of time--typically five years or more into the future. The preceding words provide a definition of--

    a. intermediate goals
    b. short-term goals
    c. long-term goals
    d. mission statements

2. Which of the following is NOT a basic step in strategy formulation?

    a. setting strategic goals
    b. analyzing the organization and its environment
    c. matching the organization and its environment
    d. devising evaluation methods for determining degree of goal accomplishment

3. The textbook relates that Coca-Cola decided to increase sales in Europe by building European bottling facilities. This was used as an illustration of--

   a. strategic planning
   b. contingency planning
   c. tactical planning
   d. environment analysis

4. This kind of planning attempts to identify in advance important aspects of a business or its market that might change. It also identifies the ways in which a company will respond to changes. Which kind of planning is it?

   a. strategic planning
   b. contingency planning
   c. tactical planning
   d. environment analysis

5. When the oil tanker Exxon Valdez spilled millions of gallons of oil off the coast of Alaska in March, 1989, Exxon went into a crisis management mode--

   a. immediately
   b. only after pressure from the Federal government
   c. more slowly than some critics would have liked
   d. only after several months of negotiations

6. Of the following firms cited in the textbook, which put forth the least effective crisis management effort?

   a. AT&T
   b. Delta
   c. Johnson & Johnson
   d. Exxon

7. Which of the following terms is NOT used in referring to the elements of the "hierarchy of plans" for an organization?

   a. strategic
   b. alternative
   c. tactical
   d. operational

8. The process of monitoring a firm's performance to make sure that it is meeting its goals is referred to as--

   a. planning
   b. organizing
   c. leading
   d. controlling

9. Which of the following positions would be classified within the category of middle managers?

    a. division manager
    b. treasurer
    c. supervisor
    d. vice president

10. Which kind of manager is responsible for hiring and training employees, evaluating performance, and determining compensation?

    a. human resources
    b. information
    c. operations
    d. marketing

11. Production is the responsibility of which kind of manager?

    a. marketing
    b. finance
    c. operations
    d. human resources

12. Although technical skills are important at all levels of management, they are _especially_ important for--

    a. first-line managers
    b. middle managers
    c. top managers
    d. members of board of directors

13. Although human relations skills are important at all levels, the textbook says they may be most important for--

    a. first-line managers
    b. middle managers
    c. top managers
    d. members of board of directors

14. Here's a statement from a manager: "Twelve years from now, every home in America will have its own computerized kitchen. The preparation of a supper can be initiated by homeward bound workers merely by sending programming signals from their vehicles as they travel on the freeway. For persons with pressing evening plans, they can pick up supper from a drive-through window at their own home. And our firm is going to make all of this possible." Such a statement is an example of the use of--

    a. technical skills
    b. conceptual skills
    c. decision-making skills
    d. human relations skills

15. When Michael Eisner became CEO of the Walt Disney Company in 1984, he realized that the company had become stagnant. In so doing, he had--

   a. defined the problem
   b. selected alternatives
   c. implemented a chosen alternative
   d. evaluated the effectiveness of his choice

16. Which of the following is least likely to be a function of an organization's corporate culture?

   a. directs employees' efforts toward the same goals
   b. helps newcomers learn accepted behaviors
   c. gives each organization its own identity
   d. provides tactical plans for implementing strategies

17. Which of the following is usually NOT considered to be a determinant of corporate culture?

   a. values
   b. history
   c. external environment
   d. stories and legends

18. What did Hyatt Hotels do for some 379 corporate employees to help them better understand the work of lower-level employees?

   a. provided a three-week seminar in New York
   b. had them make beds and carry luggage
   c. set up managerial correspondence courses
   d. had "interaction receptions" in several hotels

19. Within the area of financial management, which of the following is normally considered to be middle management?

   a. vice president for finance
   b. division controller
   c. accounting supervisor
   d. treasurer

20. As an example of corporate culture having a lasting effect on an organization, most of Ford's top executives today are still, just as was Henry Ford himself--

   a. Republicans
   b. forward thinkers
   c. "car people"
   d. market-oriented

WRITING TO LEARN

1. Go back to multiple choice question #14 and expand further on that futuristic theme, thus making use of your conceptual skills.

2. Explain why you think human relations skills are important at all levels of management. If you do not agree, then explain why they are NOT important at all levels of management.

3. Explain why conceptual skills are so important at the top-manager level and that technical skills at that level are of less importance.

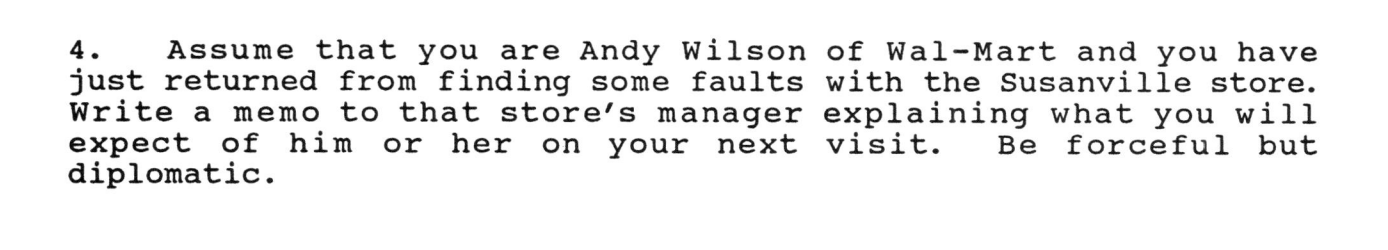

4. Assume that you are Andy Wilson of Wal-Mart and you have just returned from finding some faults with the Susanville store. Write a memo to that store's manager explaining what you will expect of him or her on your next visit. Be forceful but diplomatic.

5. Describe with numerous examples the differences between strategic plans and tactical plans of an organization.

6. You have just formed a new company that manufactures and sells sweatshirts with pictures of rock stars on them. Write a mission statement for this new firm.

7. Explain, using numerous examples, the difference between tactical plans and operational plans.

8. You are the CEO of a soft-drink corporation. Develop a memorandum that describes for your employees the procedures for crisis management in the event that a customer becomes poisoned by one of your firm's bottles of pop.

9. You have taken over a corporation that has lost large sums of money in its last two years of operation. You want to motivate the employees to turn this corporation around. What will you say to them when you meet the entire corporate working force for the first time at a mass meeting in a large auditorium?

DISCUSSION OF BUSINESS CASE 5

The key clause in this narrative is: "...Monsanto now evaluates managers on their skills in identifying, training, and promoting the women who work for them." What this clause tells us is that someone at the top has decreed that women will be given a fair chance at Monsanto. The top is where something of this nature has to start; it can't be accomplished merely because middle management thinks it is just and right. Have you ever visited a naval base or an army post? The minute you drive up to the front gate, you can tell what kind of person is commanding that installation. Is the guard at the gate sloppy and casual, or is that guard immaculately dressed, snappy, precise, and military in conduct? Are the curbs neatly whitewashed, are grassy areas recently mowed, is trash eliminated from the scene? If so, you can be sure that someone at the top cares about how things are being done at that military installation. Some of those soldiers or sailors may NOT want to be neat, but someone at the top has explained to them that they will be neat--or else! At Monsanto, for example, "Some men's initial reaction to [diversity training] is defensive." Well, such men could possibly be told in macho fashion: "Either go along with what we are doing here, or get out!" It has to start at the top. In the Navy's recent Tailhook scandal, it was alleged that perhaps the highest-ranking officer in the United States Navy knew what was happening but did nothing about it. In this case, allegedly, the top level didn't care. As a result, whether fair to that top officer or not, allegedly there was extreme pressure to get him to relinquish his spot at the top because that top officer had allegedly not provided what some critics would call ethical leadership. This all fits in with corporate culture. The textbook says: "The values of top management help set the tone of the organization." From now forth, the corporate culture at Monsanto places value on the contributions of women in its management ranks. But there is still a caution to be observed here. The new corporate culture at Monsanto may be dictating: women will be given equal opportunity, BUT a woman will never become our CEO.

1. Compare Andy Wilson's efforts to shape up the Susanville store with Monsanto's new approach to women in management.

2. Do you think that a new CEO at Monsanto could reverse this new approach of equal opportunity for women? Why or why not?

3. If every male middle manager at Monsanto campaigned for equal opportunity for women, could anything have been accomplished if the CEO and board opposed such a move?

4. Explain why "some men's initial reaction to [diversity training] is defensive" at Monsanto.

ANSWERS TO TRUE-FALSE QUESTIONS

1.	T (p. 100)		6.	T (p. 107)
2.	F (p. 101)		7.	T (p. 109)
3.	F (p. 102-103)		8.	F (p. 111)
4.	T (p. 105)		9.	F (p. 111)
5.	F (p. 106)		10.	T (p. 112)

ANSWERS TO MULTIPLE CHOICE QUESTIONS

1.	c (p. 101)		11.	c (p. 110)
2.	d (p. 102)		12.	a (p. 111)
3.	c (p. 104)		13.	b (p. 112)
4.	b (p. 105)		14.	b (p. 112-113)
5.	c (p. 105)		15.	a (p. 114)
6.	d (p. 105-106)		16.	d (p. 115)
7.	b (p. 103)		17.	c (p. 115)
8.	d (p. 107-108)		18.	b (p. 111)
9.	a (p. 109)		19.	b (p. 111)
10.	a (p. 110)		20.	c (p. 115)

CHAPTER SIX

ORGANIZING THE BUSINESS ENTERPRISE

CHAPTER OVERVIEW

Organizational structure is the specification of the jobs to be done within an organization and the ways in which those jobs relate to one another. Many elements work together to determine an organization's structure; chief among these are the organization's purpose, mission, and strategy. The first step in developing the structure of any business involves specialization and departmentalization. Departmentalization can be along customer, product, process, geographic, or functional lines. In the decision-making hierarchy, managers perform tasks by means of responsibility and authority, delegation, and accountability. In a centralized organization, most decision-making authority is held by upper-level managers; in decentralized organizations, that authority is delegated to lower levels. Three forms of authority are line, staff, and functional. Alternative organizational structures have emerged to meet changing needs: divisional, matrix, and international. Intrapreneuring is creating and maintaining the innovation and flexibility of a small-business environment within a large, bureaucratic structure. Everyday social interactions that transcend formal job interrelationships are called the informal organization, whose communication line is the grapevine.

LEARNING OBJECTIVES

1. Discuss the elements that influence a firm's organizational structure.

2. Describe specialization and departmentalization as the building blocks of organizational structure.

3. Distinguish between responsibility and authority and explain the differences in decision making in centralized and decentralized organizations.

4. Explain the differences among divisional, matrix, and international organization structures and discuss the reasons for encouraging intrapreneuring.

5. Define the informal organization and explain its importance.

DISCUSSION OF OPENING VIGNETTE

Clearly, this is a case of a firm with tight centralization going to a much looser <u>de</u>centralization. That is quite obvious. In addition, there <u>is</u> subtle evidence that some strategic soul searching took place at the same time. And this going back to square one in philosophy is necessary when reorganization is felt to be needed. In other words, the firm asks itself: "Why do we exist? When we answer that question, then we are in a position to proceed with a reorganization that is consistent with this reason for existing." Here's what we mean. Time executives could very well admit: "We are in business to sell advertising; it is this revenue that makes it possible for us to function. Gathering and interpreting news and selling subscriptions will not produce enough revenue to keep us afloat!" This basic truth is reflected in the decision to appoint a <u>seasoned advertising person</u> as the publisher of each Time, Inc. magazine. You may ask, "Why not appoint as publisher a person with great journalistic credentials?" The answer is: journalism doesn't bring in the revenue--advertising does. This is something that the broadcasting industry learned many, many years ago. Radio and TV station managers, ever since the 1930's and up to today, are predominantly from advertising backgrounds. They may not know that much about how to produce a quality radio or television program. They may not know how to hire the disc jockey with the best voice for your local station. They may not care about acquiring the most sophisticated transmission equipment. But they do know how to appeal to advertisers, and it is advertisers who provide the life blood of a local station. From the angle of authority and responsibility, the president of each magazine has an increase in both. If his or her magazine fails, the president cannot blame it on central policy. The fault is right there in the individual magazine. And presidents who cannot produce a profit could well be looking for a job elsewhere.

1. Do you sense in this reorganization a de-emphasis on quality news reporting and analysis? Why or why not?

2. With each magazine becoming independent, explore the possibility that additional staff added at each magazine will mean burdensome new salary expense that will cut into profits.

3. Now that the magazines are operating independently, what will be the fate of one of these publications if it is unable to produce a positive net income within a reasonable amount of time?

4. Explain this phrase from the narrative: "...remove the corporate hierarchy from the day-to-day management of the business."

ANNOTATED KEY TERMS

Organizational structure - The specification of the jobs to be done within an organization and the ways in which they relate to one another.

Organization chart - A diagram that depicts a company's structure and shows employees where they fit into its operations.

Chain of command - The reporting relationships within a company.

Job specialization - The process of identifying the specific jobs that need to be done and designating the people who will perform them.

Departmentalization - The process of grouping jobs into logical units.

Customer departmentalization - Departmentalization according to types of customers likely to buy a given product.

Product departmentalization - Departmentalization according to specific products being created.

Process departmentalization - Departmentalization according to production process used to create a good or service.

Geographic departmentalization - Departmentalization according to areas served by a business.

Functional departmentalization - Departmentalization according to a group's functions or activities.

Profit center - A separate company unit responsible for its own costs and profits.

Responsibility - The duty to perform an assigned task.

Authority - The power to make the decisions necessary to complete a task.

Delegation - The assignment of a task, responsibility, or authority by a manager to a subordinate.

Accountability - The liability of subordinates for accomplishing tasks assigned by managers.

Centralized organization - An organization in which most decision-making authority is held by upper-level management.

Decentralized organization - An organization in which a great deal of decision-making authority is delegated to levels of management at points below the top.

Line system - An organizational structure in which authority flows in a direct chain of command from the top of the company to the bottom.

Line department - A department directly linked to the production and sales of a specific product.

Span of control - The number of people supervised by one manager.

Staff members - The advisers and counselors who aid line departments in making decisions but who do not have the authority to make final decisions.

Line-and-staff system - An organization including both line departments and staff members who advise line managers.

Functional organization - A form of business organization in which authority is determined by the relationships between group functions and activities.

Divisional organization - An organizational structure in which corporate divisions operate as relatively autonomous businesses under the larger corporate umbrella.

Business portfolio approach - An organizational strategy by which a firm structures itself around its business units.

Division - A department that resembles a separate business in producing and marketing its own products.

Conglomerate - An organization in which divisions may be unrelated.

Matrix structure - An organizational structure in which teams are formed and team members report to two or more managers.

International organizational structures - Approaches to organizational structure developed in response to the need to manufacture, purchase, and sell in global markets.

Intrapreneuring - The process of creating and maintaining the innovation and flexibility of a small-business environment within the confines of a large organization.

Informal organization - The network, unrelated to a firm's formal authority structure, of everyday social interactions among company employees.

Grapevine - An informal communication system that carries gossip and information throughout an organization.

TRUE-FALSE QUESTIONS

1. Organizational structure is the specification of the jobs to be done within an organization and the ways in which those jobs relate to one another.

2. Departmentalization may occur along customer, product, process, geographic, or functional lines.

3. When a company develops departments according to a group's activities, then we have departmentalization by process.

4. Responsibility is the power to make the decisions necessary to complete a task.

5. If a subordinate does not perform an assigned task properly or promptly, he or she may be subject to reprimand. This is a part of the essence of accountability.

6. In a centralized organization, most decision-making authority is held by upper-level managers.

7. When we use the term "span of control," we are referring to just how much power a given manager has over his subordinates.

8. Staff employees are the "doers" and producers in a company.

9. In a conglomerate, divisions may be completely unrelated.

10. The matrix structure was pioneered by the National Aeronautical and Space Administration (NASA).

MULTIPLE CHOICE QUESTIONS

1. It is defined as the specification of the jobs to be done within an organization and the ways in which those jobs relate to one another. What is it?

    a. matrix organization
    b. span of control
    c. organizational structure
    d. chain of command

2. One of the following is NOT a way for an organization to departmentalize. Please select the inappropriate item.

    a. by process
    b. by product
    c. by customer
    d. by supplier

3. Which one of the following is given by the textbook as a way to departmentalize?

    a. by supplier
    b. by customer
    c. by volume
    d. by direction

4. It begins when a manager assigns a task to a subordinate. What is it?

    a. delegation
    b. chain of command
    c. matrix
    d. strategy

5. In the normal organization, a manager's responsibility should be greater than his or her authority--

    a. most of the time
    b. occasionally
    c. almost never
    d. never

6. Decentralization is most likely to be found in--

    a. a new sole proprietorship
    b. a small business
    c. a very large firm
    d. a firm desiring a great degree of standardization

7. Which of the following is the best match for true delegation of authority and responsibility?

    a. centralized organization
    b. very narrow span of control
    c. greatly decentralized firm
    d. Dillard's Department Stores

8. Which of the following firms has a long history of decentralization, according to your textbook?

    a. General Electric
    b. Dillard's Department Stores
    c. McDonald's
    d. Time, Inc.

9. Which of the following groups would more than likely be considered as "staff" in a line-and-staff system at a manufacturing firm?

    a. distribution
    b. accountants
    c. sales
    d. painting

10. Which of the following groups would more than likely be considered as "line" in a line-and-staff system?

    a. accountants
    b. lawyers
    c. human resources
    d. sales

11. A given organization has a finance department, a marketing department, an operations department, etc. From these facts alone, then, we can conclude that this organization can be referred to as a--

    a. functional organization
    b. line-and-staff system
    c. a firm with broad span of control
    d. departmentalized firm

12. Departments resemble separate businesses in that they produce and market their own products. The head of each such department may be a corporate vice president, or even a president. This grouping is referred to as--

    a. conglomerate
    b. line-and-staff system
    c. divisional organization
    d. intrapreneuring

13. In a large organization with large divisions within it, the divisions may be completely unrelated. The term for such an organization is--

    a. divisional establishment
    b. conglomerate
    c. accountable units
    d. systemic

14. Teams are formed in which individuals report to two or more managers, usually including a line manager and a staff manager. These are some of the characteristics of the organization called--

    a. matrix
    b. systemic
    c. conglomerate
    d. line chain

15. Your project manager may demand that you work on one aspect of a proposal while your department manager wants you to work on another. This is a situation that is likely to pop up in which of the following?

   a. matrix
   b. systemic
   c. conglomerate
   d. line chain

16. Sometimes in large organizations, large, cumbersome, bureaucratic structures can develop that are stifling to creativity and innovation. A way to combat this is--

   a. line-and-staff system
   b. divisional organization
   c. greater centralization
   d. intrapreneuring

17. Eileen Bedell of New York Banker's Trust Company is to be associated with--

   a. line-and-staff system
   b. divisional organization
   c. greater centralization
   d. intrapreneuring

18. The communication system utilized by the informal organization is referred to as the--

   a. information superhighway
   b. grapevine
   c. fiber optic network
   d. company newspaper

19. Which of the following is a negative aspect of the informal organization, according to your textbook?

   a. reinforcement of office politics
   b. solving of organizational problems
   c. informal interaction
   d. increased flow of ideas

20. Which of the following is NOT true of the communication system of the informal organization?

   a. a useful source of information
   b. usually supplies information more slowly than official channels
   c. can carry inaccurate information
   d. carries advance word of impending changes

WRITING TO LEARN

1. Assemble as many as you can of the positive aspects of the informal organization and write about them.

2. Tell why you think that a top-level manager should or should not feed official information through the grapevine of his or her organization.

3. Pick any two of the methods for departmentalizing an organization and describe them with a generous supply of examples.

4. Explain the difference between process departmentalization and functional departmentalization.

5. Even though you may feel that the matrix system is a wonderful organizational innovation, give several complete reasons why the matrix is a very bad idea.

6. Explain, with examples, what problems can develop when a middle manager has been given responsibility that is far less than equivalent to the authority he or she has been awarded.

7. Often the term "accountability" is difficult to define. Nevertheless, make an attempt at doing so, with a liberal use of examples.

8. Assume that it is possible to decentralize too far. Explain how this can happen and indicate what are the negative consequences of such a development.

9. In as complete a fashion as possible, explain the difference between the terms "line" and "staff."

DISCUSSION OF BUSINESS CASE 6

This narrative fortunately provides new insights into what decentralization is all about. First, you will note that there is mention that Johnson & Johnson has a "relatively flat organizational structure." This means that spans of control will be broad. Let's check that out mathematically. There are 166 operating company presidents. They report to 19 group chairpersons. This means the average chairperson, then, has 8.7 presidents--let's round it off at 9--in his or her span of control. Such a span pretty well dictates that strong delegating of both authority and responsibility has to take place. Otherwise, a group chairperson will be looking over the shoulders of 9 presidents. Keeping up with the inner workings of 9 companies is too much to ask; the group chairperson must leave problems in the hands of those presidents. Second, notice that having 166 companies operating strictly on their own has led to the maintaining of 166 managerial staffs and thus to greater overhead costs for Johnson & Johnson as a whole. This is the negative side of decentralization. Third, notice that Johnson & Johnson CEO Ralph S. Larsen is altering the organization a bit at the present time, bringing in a little more centralization. Even though much of the case sings the praises of decentralization, we must remember that this approach was launched in the 1930's. Great as it may have been back then, it's possible that what is left of the 1990's and the third millennium A.D. to come are going to be calling for a totally different approach. And so, Johnson & Johnson is in a state of flux currently as Mr. Larsen reworks the organization. We must step in to defend Mr. Larsen because he is willing to survey the environment in which Johnson & Johnson exists and then to adjust to that ever-changing environment. This flexibility, this ability to look ahead, this willingness to make whatever changes are necessary will continue to characterize the great and successful companies.

1. Do you feel that it would be possible for Mr. Larsen to direct all 166 company presidents to cut their staffs by fifty percent in order to reduce overhead? Why or why not?

2. Comment upon this statement: "Decentralization has worked for us since the 1930's, and there's no reason that it won't continue to be appropriate."

3. As Mr. Larsen sets about making some changes in the organization, what advice would you offer him?

4. What are some reasons why Johnson & Johnson is NOT at the moment considering further decentralization?

ANSWERS TO TRUE-FALSE QUESTIONS

1.	T (p. 125-126)	6.	T (p. 133)
2.	T (p. 128)	7.	F (p. 134)
3.	F (p. 129)	8.	F (p. 135)
4.	F (p. 131)	9.	T (p. 137)
5.	T (p. 131)	10.	T (p. 137)

ANSWERS TO MULTIPLE CHOICE QUESTIONS

1.	c (p. 125-126)	11.	a (p. 136)
2.	d (p. 128-129)	12.	c (p. 136)
3.	b (p. 129)	13.	b (p. 137)
4.	a (p. 131)	14.	a (p. 137)
5.	d (p. 131)	15.	a (p. 140)
6.	c (p. 133)	16.	d (p. 141)
7.	c (p. 133-134)	17.	d (p. 142)
8.	a (p. 134)	18.	c (p. 143-144)
9.	b (p. 135)	19.	a (p. 143)
10.	d (p. 135)	20.	b (p. 143-144)

CHAPTER SEVEN

RUNNING THE SMALL BUSINESS

CHAPTER OVERVIEW

Since it is difficult to define a small business in numerical terms, it can be defined simply as one which is independently owned and managed and which does not dominate its market. The contribution of small business can be seen in terms of its effect on key aspects of the U.S. economic system: job creation, innovation, and big business. Small businesses fall into five major industry groups: services, retailing, wholesaling, manufacturing, and agriculture. Reasons for small business failure are: managerial incompetence; neglect; weak control systems; and insufficient capital. Reasons for success are: hard work; market demand for the products or services provided; managerial competence; and luck. A small business can be started by buying out an existing business or by starting from scratch. Risks are greater in the latter approach. Small businesses can be financed by the owner's own funds, by friends of the owner, by banks, independent investors, government loans, venture capital firms, small-business investment companies, foreign investors, and asset-based lenders. An incubator is a sheltered environment for new businesses that generally includes cost-sharing and other subsidies. There are several sources of management advice, and franchising can often be appropriate for small businesses.

LEARNING OBJECTIVES

1. Define small business and explain its importance to the U.S. economy.

2. Explain which types of enterprise best lend themselves to small-business success.

3. Identify the key reasons for the success and failure of small businesses.

4. Describe the start-up decisions made by small businesses and identify sources of financial aid and management advice available to such enterprises.

5. Identify the advantages and disadvantages of franchising.

DISCUSSION OF OPENING VIGNETTE

There is in Sheri Poe's story something very familiar, and that is the struggle for recognition. When a small business entrepreneur is trying to launch a new business, investors are needed. But to place money and faith in a new venture, investors must <u>recognize</u> that this new entrepreneur has something that is really going to sell. Getting this recognition from investors is very difficult, and some entrepreneurs never pull off the trick. But this struggle for recognition occurs in all areas. In 1923, the manager of a minor league baseball team in Hartford, Connecticut, wanted to fire young Lou Gehrig because the manager thought that future baseball immortal Gehrig had no potential. When Albert Einstein finished high school, he was not admitted to the college he wanted because his grades weren't good enough. Elderly comedian George Burns was just a minor vaudeville performer for several decades before someone "discovered" him. Chester F. Carlson invented something in the late 1930's. No major company was interested in his idea, although he approached the corporate giants of America. Finally, a firm in Rochester, New York took a chance on Carlson's idea and began to market it. That firm is known today as the Xerox Corporation. When Charles Babbage died in 1873, a lot of people thought his ideas qualified him as an eccentric idiot. But today, we refer to Babbage as the father of the computer. Basically, regardless of what you may have heard, the world is NOT looking for new ideas or new talent. Someone has to come along and force on us these new ideas and new talents. That's what Sheri Poe did. But notice that she did it with persistence. We can imagine that she devoted her every waking minute back in the 1980's to getting some investor to believe in her concept. Every waking minute; it wasn't something she did on a part-time basis. We must also note that she was creative. She proved this by seeking out investors who had turned down Peter Fireman of Reebok, saying to them in essence, "You blew it last time. I've come here to give you a second chance."

1. Did being a woman help or hinder Sheri Poe in getting her firm launched? Explain your answer.

2. Supposing the investors mentioned in the narrative had turned her down, where else could Sheri Poe have turned?

3. You are Sheri Poe. Respond to this statement from a potential lender: "My dear, there are already too many sneaker manufacturers!"

4. Many CEOs are pretty well anonymous and behind the scenes. What are some advantages or disadvantages of keeping the personality of Sheri Poe out in front of the public at all times?

ANNOTATED KEY TERMS

Small Business Administration (SBA) - Federal agency charged with assisting small businesses.

Small business - Independently owned and managed business that does not dominate its market.

Entrepreneur - Businessperson who accepts both the risks and opportunities in creating and operating a new business venture.

Innovations - New ways of using resources in the creation of products or processes.

Lifestyle business - Business formed for the specific purpose of allowing its owner to spend his or her time, energy, and money in a certain way.

High-growth venture - Business that has rapid growth as its basic goal from the start.

Venture capital firm - Group of small investors that invests money in companies with rapid growth potential.

Small-business investment company (SBIC) - Federally licensed company that borrows money from the SBA to invest in or loan to small businesses.

Minority enterprise small business investment company (MESBIC) - Federally sponsored company that specializes in financing businesses owned and operated by minorities.

Guaranteed loans program - Program in which the SBA guarantees to repay 75 to 85 percent of small business commercial loans up to $750,000.

Immediate participation loans program - Program in which small businesses are loaned funds put up jointly by banks and the SBA.

Local development companies (LDCs) program - Program in which the SBA works with local for-profit or nonprofit organizations seeking to boost a community's economy.

Incubator - "Sheltered environment" for new businesses that generally includes cost sharing and other subsidies.

Management consultant - Independent outside specialist hired to help managers solve business problems.

Service Corps of Retired Executives (SCORE) - SBA program in which retired executives work with small businesses on a volunteer basis.

Active Corps of Executives (ACE) - SBA program in which currently employed executives work with small businesses on a volunteer basis.

Small Business Institute (SBI) - SBA program in which college and university students and instructors work with small businesspeople to help solve specific problems.

Small Business Development Center (SBDC) - SBA program designed to consolidate information from various disciplines and to make it available to small businesses.

Networking - Interactions among businesspeople for the purpose of discussing mutual problems, solutions, and opportunities.

Franchise - An arrangement in which a buyer (franchisee) purchases the right to sell the good or service of the seller (franchiser).

TRUE-FALSE QUESTIONS

1. The textbook has indicated that to be considered a small business a firm must employ ten persons or less and have an annual net income of $150,000 or less.

2. A small business can be defined simply as one which is independently owned and managed and which does not dominate its market.

3. Most of the products made by big manufacturers are sold to consumers by small businesses.

4. Services are the largest and fastest growing segment of small business enterprise.

5. The textbook has indicated that the small farmer has just about been eliminated from the U.S. economy.

6. Unfortunately, 60 percent of all new businesses will not celebrate a sixth anniversary.

7. Although at one time managerial incompetence was a major cause of small business failure, it is no longer a factor in such failure.

8. Luck is listed as a reason for the success of a small business.

9. The risks from buying an existing firm are greater than those associated with starting a new firm from scratch.

10. Obtaining money from a venture capital firm is very difficult because venture capital firms as a rule invest only in those firms that have eliminated all the risks involved in getting a small business started.

MULTIPLE CHOICE QUESTIONS

1. In defining a small business, only one of the characteristics below is appropriate. Which is it?

    a. employs fewer than 63 employees
    b. must be affiliated with a major corporation
    c. does not dominate its market
    d. cannot earn annual income over $910,000

2. Which of the following is NOT listed by the textbook as being impacted by American small business?

   a. government
   b. job creation
   c. big business
   d. innovation

3. Which of the following items is least characteristic of the typical small business entrepreneur?

   a. accepts risks
   b. accepts opportunities
   c. can be a maverick
   d. is cautious

4. Which one of the following is among the five major small-business industry groups?

   a. military
   b. retailing
   c. space
   d. entertainment

5. Which one of the following is NOT among the five major small-business industry groups?

   a. manufacturing
   b. retailing
   c. agriculture
   d. entertainment

6. Which one of the following is among the five major small-business industry groups?

   a. wholesaling
   b. military
   c. space
   d. transportation

7. The textbook provides the case of Marc Friedland who is a 30-year-old designer, manufacturer, and retailer for upscale clientele. What is Friedland's product?

   a. fresh fruit baskets
   b. home motion picture studios
   c. engraved stationery
   d. sporting goods

8. Which of the following does the textbook label as perhaps the oldest small business enterprise?

   a. retailing
   b. agriculture
   c. manufacturing
   d. services

9. The textbook has treated several computer firms that started as small businesses. They are listed below along with an inappropriate item. Indicate the item that does not fit in this list.

   a. IBM
   b. Dell
   c. Microsoft
   d. Compaq

10. Which of the following phrases best describes the failure rate among small businesses in recent years.

    a. almost nonexistent
    b. rising
    c. declining
    d. consistent and steady since 1987

11. Which one of the following is provided by the textbook as a reason for small business failure?

    a. managerial incompetence
    b. managerial burnout
    c. poorly directed advertising
    d. bloated inventory

12. Which one of the following is provided by the textbook as a reason for small business failure?

    a. managerial burnout
    b. transportation delays
    c. insufficient capital
    d. control systems that are too tight

13. Which one of the following is NOT provided by the textbook as a reason for small business failure?

    a. managerial incompetence
    b. neglect
    c. weak control systems
    d. too few employees

14. Which one of the following is provided by the textbook as a reason for small business success?

    a. adequate staff
    b. luck
    c. efficient transportation networks
    d. creative managerial use of time away from work

15. Which one of the following is provided by the textbook as a reason for small business success?

    a. market demand for your products or services
    b. reserve capital funds
    c. delegation
    d. wise departmentalizing of the organization

16. Which one of the following is NOT provided by the textbook as a reason for small business success?

    a. ethics of the manager
    b. managerial competence
    c. luck
    d. hard work, drive, and dedication

17. They are groups of small investors seeking to make profits on companies with rapid growth potential. Most of them do not lend money; rather they invest it, supplying money in return for stock. What are they called?

    a. incubators
    b. SBDCs
    c. MESBICs
    d. venture capital firms

18. They specialize in financing businesses owned and operated by minorities. What are they?

    a. incubators
    b. SBDCs
    c. MESBICs
    d. venture capital firms

19. Through one of these, new businesses may be leased office space at below-market rates, and they may share receptionists, typing personnel, copying facilities, supply rooms, and a parking lot. What do you call one of these?

    a. SBA
    b. incubator
    c. SCORE
    d. consultancy

20. Which of the following is listed by the textbook as perhaps the most significant disadvantage of franchising as a small business venture?

    a. access to big-business management skills
    b. independence
    c. business is established virtually overnight
    d. start-up cost

WRITING TO LEARN

1. Explain what you feel is the most important step to take if you are considering opening your own small business.

2. Select any one of the reasons the textbook has given for small business success and explain it fully, using plenty of illustrations.

3. Look again at the Opening Vignette and the saga of Sheri Poe. What is the quality possessed by Ms. Poe that must be present, in your opinion, for success in small business?

4. The textbook has indicated that the existence of a market for your product or service is essential for small business success. Explain how you would go about determining the readiness of a market to receive your brand-new product.

5. Expand upon what the book suggests about the remaining presence of the small-scale farmer in the United States and of his or her importance in our economy.

6. The textbook indicates that small business has an impact on big business. Explain thoroughly what this means and develop several good examples of this impact.

7. Select any one of the reasons the textbook has given for small business failure. Expand upon it, explain it, and give as many illustrations as possible.

8. Look again at the list of reasons for small business failure provided by the textbook. To this list add, explain, and illustrate a reason of your own that has not been addressed by the textbook.

9. Do you agree that luck should be listed as a factor in success of a small business? If you do, then explain in great detail why this is so. If you do not, then explain in great detail why luck should NOT be included in such a list of success factors.

DISCUSSION OF BUSINESS CASE 7

This KFC case beautifully illustrates several key points from this chapter in the textbook. First of all, be reminded that the text indicated that a reason for small business success is "market demand for the products or services being provided." If an entrepreneur's market research shows that nobody wants the product he or she is about to sell, then that entrepreneur should alter plans. Likewise, KFC was not about to offer rotisserie chicken at its facilities across the nation until the central office was certain that rotisserie chicken would be popular. So, KFC "began test-marketing rotisserie chickens" in several of their outlets. National franchise operations are doing this testing all the time. For example, you might call a friend at a location clear across the country and say that you really enjoyed a McStrawberry Fliggenhammer (as a ridiculous example) at a McDonald's. Your friend will laugh and say, "You're putting me on. McDonald's doesn't have a McStrawberry Fliggenhammer." What's occurring is that the Fliggenhammer is being test-marketed in your area only. If the Fliggenhammer does NOT go over very well in your area, it will soon cease to appear. If it's a hit in your test-market area, your friend far away will soon be able to get one at his or her location. Second, we see how franchising works by noting that John Marsella could not go ahead and feature in his KFC restaurants what he knew was a smash hit with people in his part of the country. And it took a while before the KFC wheels could get turning in the direction of this innovation. Third, we note again that markets and people are constantly changing, and KFC must adapt. Today, there is great concern not only about calories but also about cholesterol--said to be a major cause of heart difficulties. If KFC's customers are becoming alarmed about cholesterol, then KFC must do something about it. Sticking to the Colonel's original "soaked in oil" chicken recipe could mean a drop in sales among health-conscious Americans.

1. Explain why John Marsella did not go ahead and install rotisseries in his KFC restaurant.

2. React to this statement: "All this cholesterol emphasis is looney. If people like chicken the way we've always fried it, they won't let a little cholesterol stand in their way."

3. If people in John Marsella's New Jersey KFC outlets loved rotisserie chicken and bought it frequently but people in Alabama, Texas, and Nevada detested it, do you feel that KFC should offer it in some restaurants and not in others? Why or why not?

4. Explain why test-marketing a potential new product is so important.

ANSWERS TO TRUE-FALSE QUESTIONS

1. F (p. 151)
2. T (p. 151)
3. T (p. 153)
4. T (p. 154)
5. F (p. 155)
6. T (p. 156)
7. F (p. 157)
8. T (p. 159)
9. F (p. 162)
10. F (p. 164)

ANSWERS TO MULTIPLE CHOICE QUESTIONS

1. c (p. 151)
2. a (p. 152-153)
3. d (p. 153)
4. b (p. 154)
5. d (p. 154)
6. a (p. 154)
7. c (p. 154)
8. b (p. 155)
9. a (p. 156)
10. c (p. 156)
11. a (p. 157)
12. c (p. 157)
13. d (p. 157)
14. b (p. 158)
15. a (p. 158)
16. a (p. 158)
17. d (p. 163-164)
18. c (p. 164)
19. b (p. 165)
20. d (p. 169-170)

CHAPTER EIGHT

MOTIVATING, SATISFYING, AND LEADING EMPLOYEES

CHAPTER OVERVIEW

The foundation of good human relations is a satisfied workforce. Job satisfaction is the degree of enjoyment that people derive from performing their jobs. Morale is the overall attitude that employees have toward their workplace. Motivation is the set of forces that cause people to behave in certain ways. Three approaches to human relations in the workplace are: classical theory and scientific management; behavior theory; and motivational theory. Theory X managers tend to believe that people are naturally lazy and uncooperative. Theory Y managers tend to believe that people are naturally energetic and are interested in being productive. The five levels of Maslow's hierarchy of needs are: physiological; security; social; esteem; and self-actualization. Leadership is the process of motivating others to work to meet specific objectives. Three leadership styles are autocratic, democratic, and free-rein. Managers have started to view appropriate managerial behavior as contingent upon the elements unique to the situation. Management by objectives (MBO) is a system of collaborative goal setting. Other approaches to job satisfaction are job enrichment, job design, modified work schedules, telecommuting, and work sharing.

LEARNING OBJECTIVES

1. Discuss the importance of job satisfaction and employee morale and summarize their roles in human relations in the workplace.

2. Identify and summarize the most important theories of employee motivation.

3. Discuss different managerial styles of leadership and their impact on human relations in the workplace.

4. Describe some of the strategies used by organizations to improve employee motivation and job satisfaction.

DISCUSSION OF OPENING VIGNETTE

No doubt about it, Jack Smith is making a difference at General Motors. And in this chapter we focus not so much on solving financial problems but on Smith's efforts at motivating, satisfying, and leading employees. You will notice that Smith encourages "participation, delegation, and openness." When we hear such things, we need to be cautious. We'll assume that Smith is indeed sincere in bringing such changes to General Motors. However, there have been managers in years past, in many organizations, who have claimed to be instituting "participation, delegation, and openness" but who in reality were encouraging none of these three. Such a manager could be caught saying to his or her inner circle: "I don't want employees participating in my decisions, I just want them to THINK they are participating. That's the trick." Usually, employees will soon catch on to such managers. Jack Smith, fortunately, is succeeding because his actions back up his words. Closing the executive dining room was one of those actions. Notice also that he--at this writing--is getting along well with the United Auto Workers Union. Having a cooperative relationship with the unions at his or her firm is very important to a manager's success. Labor-management relations can often be stormy, but some firms have been able to avoid such clashes. What would have been interesting to hear is the final conversation between Jack Smith and the GM board as the latter awarded the job to Smith. Keeping in mind the sweeping, even cataclysmic changes that Smith has been able to make at GM, we can imagine that Smith must have said to the board: "If I take this job, I want full authority to tear this place apart and then reassemble it my way. Is that clear? When I make a change, I don't want any board member calling me and telling me I can't do it. Is that clear?" And we can imagine a board chairman saying: "You've got our word on it, Jack. Go ahead!" If that's the way it really happened, then Jack Smith is enjoying a unique situation. What's more, he's making the most of it!

1. From what you have read, do you feel that Jack Smith really believes in "participation, delegation, and openness"? Why or why not?

2. When numerous GM employees have to be cut from the payroll, what effect do you feel this has on those who are allowed to remain as employees?

3. Based on this case narrative, what do you see as the drawbacks of so many committees functioning within General Motors? On the other hand, what is gained by having these standing committees?

4. Guess at and substantiate your guess as to how many hours per week Jack Smith works at General Motors.

ANNOTATED KEY TERMS

<u>Human relations</u> - Interactions between employers and employees and their attitudes toward one another.

<u>Job satisfaction</u> - The degree of enjoyment that people derive from performing their jobs.

<u>Morale</u> - The overall attitude that employees have toward their workplace.

<u>Motivation</u> - The set of forces that cause people to behave in certain ways.

<u>Classical theory of motivation</u> - The theory holding that workers are motivated solely by money.

<u>Scientific management</u> - The theory of management that uses scientific analysis of individual jobs to increase productivity and efficiency.

<u>Time-and-motion studies</u> - Scientific management studies using industrial engineering techniques to analyze each facet of a job to determine how to perform it most efficiently.

<u>Piecework system</u> - A system of compensation in which individuals are paid a set rate per piece completed.

<u>Hawthorne effect</u> - The tendency for productivity to increase when workers believe that they are receiving special attention from management.

<u>Theory X</u> - The theory of motivation holding that people are naturally irresponsible and uncooperative.

<u>Theory Y</u> - The theory of motivation holding that people are naturally responsible and growth-oriented, self-motivated, and interested in being productive.

<u>Hierarchy of human needs</u> - The theory of motivation describing five levels of human needs and arguing that basic needs must be filled before people work to satisfy higher-level needs.

<u>Two-factor theory</u> - The theory of motivation holding that job satisfaction depends on two types of factors: hygiene and motivating.

<u>Expectancy theory</u> - The theory of motivation holding that people are motivated to work toward rewards that they want and which they believe they have a reasonable chance of obtaining.

<u>Theory Z</u> - A management approach blending the successful elements of traditional U.S. management with the successful elements of traditional Japanese management.

Leadership - The process of motivating others to work to meet specific objectives.

Managerial style - Patterns of behavior that a manager exhibits in dealing with subordinates.

Autocratic style - A managerial style in which managers generally issue orders and expect them to be obeyed without question.

Democratic style - A managerial style in which managers generally ask for input from subordinates but retain final decision-making power.

Free-rein style - A managerial style in which managers typically serve as advisers to subordinates who are allowed to make decisions.

Contingency approach - An approach to managerial style holding that the appropriate behavior in any situation is dependent (contingent) on the elements unique to that situation.

Reinforcement - The theory that behavior can be encouraged or discouraged by means of rewards or punishments, respectively.

Management by objectives (MBO) - A set of procedures involving both managers and subordinates in setting goals and evaluating progress.

Participative management - A method of increasing job satisfaction by giving employees a voice in the management of their jobs and the company.

Job enrichment - A method of increasing job satisfaction by adding one or more motivating factors to job activities.

Job redesign - A method of increasing job satisfaction by designing a more satisfactory fit between workers and their jobs.

Flextime programs - A method of increasing job satisfaction by allowing workers to adjust work schedules on a daily or weekly basis.

Telecommuting - A form of flextime that allows people to perform some or all of a job away from standard office settings.

Work sharing (job sharing) - A method of increasing job satisfaction by allowing two or more people to share a single full-time job.

TRUE-FALSE QUESTIONS

1. Human relations is defined as the interactions between employers and employees and their attitudes toward one another.

2. Broadly speaking, job satisfaction refers to the degree of satisfaction that a manager derives from a subordinate's accomplishment of a specific task.

3. Motivation is defined as the set of forces that cause people to behave in certain ways.

4. According to the classical theory of motivation, workers are more motivated by pleasant work surroundings than by monetary compensation.

5. The theory behind time-and-motion studies pretty well contradicted and replaced everything that scientific management had proposed.

6. The now-famous Hawthorne studies were directed by Dr. Angelo J. Hawthorne of Harvard University.

7. In the Hawthorne studies, even <u>lower</u> lighting levels improved productivity.

8. Managers who subscribe to Theory X tend to believe that people are naturally lazy and uncooperative and must therefore be either punished or rewarded to be made productive.

9. The two-factor theory was developed by psychologist Abraham Maslow.

10. Leadership has been defined as the quality to inspire workers and increase their job satisfaction, with a very limited emphasis on achieving objectives.

MULTIPLE CHOICE QUESTIONS

1. It is defined as the overall attitude that employees have toward their workplace. What is it?

    a. motivation
    b. Theory Y
    c. morale
    d. classical theory

2. According to the so-called classical theory of motivation, workers are motivated solely by--

    a. satisfaction on the job
    b. threats
    c. physical conditions at the workplace
    d. money

3. What name do we associate with scientific management?

   a. Abraham Maslow
   b. Frederick Taylor
   c. Frederick Herzberg
   d. Angelo Hawthorne

4. One of the items in the list below is least related to scientific management. Please identify the inappropriate item.

   a. telecommuting
   b. time-and-motion studies
   c. quota
   d. differential percent system

5. The original intent of the Hawthorne studies in 1925 was to examine the relationship between worker output and--

   a. changes in the physical environment
   b. changes in monetary compensation
   c. changes in length of work day
   d. changes in managerial style

6. A manager says: "These are the most conscientious people I have ever managed. They are self-motivated, come in early and leave late. They devote their whole souls to this company." These remarks are consistent with--

   a. Theory X
   b. Theory Y
   c. Theory Z
   d. scientific management

7. Which one of the following items is included in Abraham Maslow's hierarchy of needs?

   a. motivational
   b. psychological
   c. physiological
   d. inspirational

8. Which one of the following items is NOT included in Abraham Maslow's hierarchy of needs?

   a. motivational
   b. social
   c. physiological
   d. esteem

9. Which one of the following items is included in Abraham Maslow's hierarchy of needs?

   a. motivating
   b. hygiene
   c. attention
   d. self-actualization

10. Workers will be dissatisfied if they believe that they have poor working conditions. If working conditions are improved, according to two-factor theory, the workers will be--

   a. satisfied
   b. still dissatisfied
   c. not dissatisfied
   d. unaware that conditions have improved

11. It is defined as the process of motivating others to work to meet specific objectives. What is it?

   a. motivation
   b. management by objectives
   c. management style
   d. leadership

12. Which of the following is NOT a management style treated by the textbook in this chapter?

   a. autocratic
   b. paternalistic
   c. free-rein
   d. democratic

13. In which of the management styles does a manager issue orders and expect them to be obeyed without question?

   a. autocratic
   b. paternalistic
   c. free-rein
   d. democratic

14. What do we have when a manager serves as an adviser to subordinates and the subordinates are allowed to make decisions?

   a. management by objectives
   b. Theory Y in practice
   c. free-rein
   d. telecommuting

15. Managers have started to view appropriate managerial behavior in any situation as dependent on the elements unique to that particular situation. This new approach is referred to as--

    a. Theory Z
    b. Theory W
    c. environmental
    d. contingency

16. When Steelcase pays "piecework rewards" to its employees, it is applying one aspect of the concept known as--

    a. scientific management
    b. job rotation
    c. contingency
    d. reinforcement

17. The National Football League (NFL) fines or suspends players found guilty of substance abuse. Which of the concepts below most closely relates to this action by the NFL?

    a. contingency
    b. autocratic
    c. reinforcement
    d. flexible pay

18. Alfie Kohn has offered four reasons why incentive plans fail. Three of these reasons are listed below along with an inappropriate item. Please identify the out-of-place item.

    a. rewards punish
    b. rewards are arriving too late
    c. rewards interfere with teamwork
    d. rewards discourage risk taking

19. In which one of the following approaches are employees given a voice in how they do their jobs and how the company is managed?

    a. participative management
    b. free-rein
    c. democratic
    d. Theory Y

20. In a firm that has been highly-innovative in catering to the satisfaction of its workers, Sue needs to coordinate quickly with Joe. However, she learns that Joe has left work for the day. Sue's frustration at not being able to contact her colleague is the result of--

    a. reinforcement
    b. self-actualization
    c. the Hawthorne effect
    d. flexible hours

WRITING TO LEARN

1. Explain what happened in the Hawthorne studies of 1925 and indicate why the Hawthorne effect is so significant.

2. What are the various flexibility programs? Which of them seems to you to be the least practical? Why?

3. What is reinforcement in a work setting? Explain Alfie Kohn's dissatisfaction with some aspects of such programs.

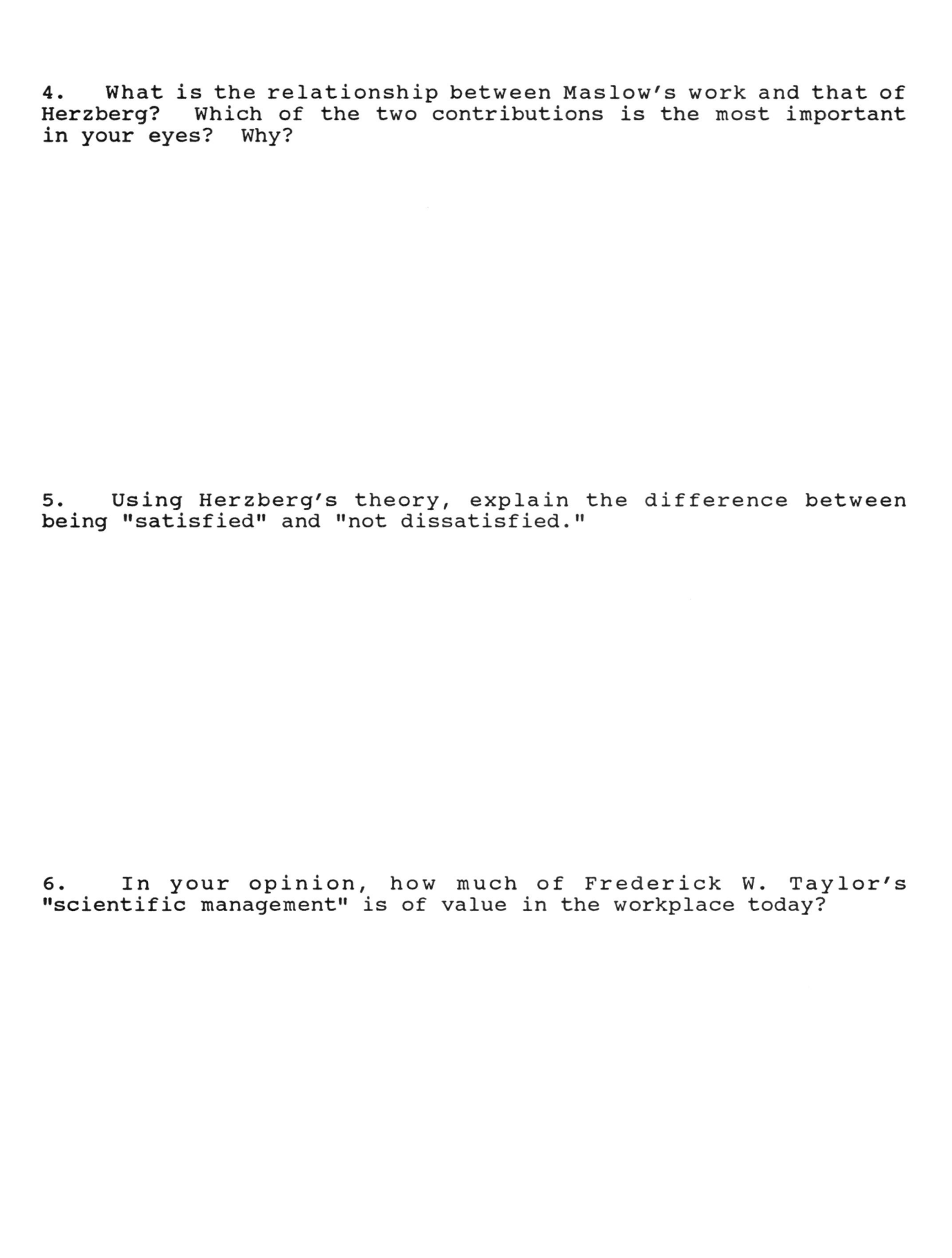

4. What is the relationship between Maslow's work and that of Herzberg? Which of the two contributions is the most important in your eyes? Why?

5. Using Herzberg's theory, explain the difference between being "satisfied" and "not dissatisfied."

6. In your opinion, how much of Frederick W. Taylor's "scientific management" is of value in the workplace today?

7. Define completely the concepts of Theory X, Theory Y, and Theory Z.

8. With the previous WRITING TO LEARN topic in mind, obviously we are now ready for Theory W. Propose a totally innovative managerial concept to be called Theory W.

9. Define, in your own terms, what is meant by the contingency approach. Develop several examples to illustrate the concept.

DISCUSSION OF BUSINESS CASE 8

The case narrative gives the impression that no one in management with the United States Postal Service has ever read anything that appears in this chapter of the textbook. Postal Service managers are depicted as strong supporters of Theory X and are portrayed as users of the autocratic management style who understand only the punishment aspect of reinforcement. However, let us be quick to recognize that the U.S. Postal Service is not the only employer that might appear to the outside casual observer to have total disregard for the various enlightenments found in this chapter. Most of us have worked--even if ever so briefly--for an autocratic manager. Despite all that is known now about motivating and satisfying employees, such managers still exist. How do we go about eliminating such managers when an organization's corporate culture dictates that the autocratic style is okay? On the other hand, a firm can become so immersed in the game of keeping happy employees that the work is not being done. The textbook suggests that keeping track of employees on flexible hours can be very difficult and that in such circumstances, some employees will fail to actually put in the required total time at work. Remember that Theory X didn't just come out of nowhere; there are, indeed, _some_ workers who are basically lazy and unmotivated. Perhaps the problem, then, with an autocratic, Theory X manager is that he or she tends to treat _all_ employees as if they were lazy, and that is a major mistake. Is it fair to label Theory X firms as "militaristic" or to say that they treat their employees as "Army recruits"? This may be unfair, since some of the best military leaders understand much of what is in this chapter, and even seemingly hard-hearted drill instructors know how to successfully and properly motivate their recruits without sole reliance on autocratic methods. But how can things be improved in the Postal Service? Remember Jack Smith in the Opening Vignette? Maybe he could come in and make a difference. Or maybe the task and the environment are too big for just one innovator.

1. Some of the positions in the U.S. Postal Service have been referred to as "political appointments." Does this or does this not complicate the task of changing leadership styles within the service? Explain.

2. Do you think it is fair and accurate to label all autocratic management as "militaristic"? Why or why not?

3. Evaluate this statement: "If we let up on the workers, we'll never get the job done."

4. Which insights gained in the Hawthorne studies of 1925 do you feel would be of help in dealing with the United States Postal Service?

ANSWERS TO TRUE-FALSE QUESTIONS

1.	T (p. 179)		6.	F	(p. 184)
2.	F (p. 180)		7.	T	(p. 184)
3.	T (p. 183)		8.	T	(p. 186)
4.	F (p. 184)		9.	F	(p. 186-187)
5.	F (p. 184)		10.	F	(p. 188)

ANSWERS TO MULTIPLE CHOICE QUESTIONS

1.	c (p. 180)		11.	d	(p. 188)
2.	d (p. 184)		12.	b	(p. 188-189)
3.	b (p. 184)		13.	a	(p. 188-189)
4.	a (p. 184)		14.	c	(p. 189)
5.	a (p. 184)		15.	d	(p. 189)
6.	b (p. 186)		16.	d	(p. 190)
7.	c (p. 186)		17.	c	(p. 191)
8.	a (p. 186)		18.	b	(p. 193)
9.	d (p. 186)		19.	a	(p. 191)
10.	c (p. 187)		20.	d	(p. 197)

CHAPTER NINE

MANAGING HUMAN RESOURCES AND LABOR RELATIONS

CHAPTER OVERVIEW

Human resource management is the development and administration of programs to enhance the quality and performance of people working in an organization. Job analysis is an evaluation of the duties required by a particular job and the qualities required to perform it. External staffing involves recruitment and selection. Internal staffing occurs through promotion or transfer of existing employees. Developing the workforce also involves orientation, training/development, performance appraisal, demotion and separation. Downsizing is defined as consolidating internal operations to make them more flexible and productive. The compensation system is the total package that a firm offers employees in return for their labor. Included in the compensation system: wages and salaries; incentive programs; and benefits programs. Legal and ethical issues in human resource management include: equal opportunity employment; equal pay and comparable worth; OSHA; employment at will; and managing workforce diversity. Collective bargaining is the process in which union leaders and managers negotiate terms of employment. The major labor law of the land today is the Labor-Management Relations Act of 1947, known as Taft-Hartley. A union becomes certified upon a majority vote of the workers affected. A strike occurs when employees temporarily walk off the job.

LEARNING OBJECTIVES

1. Define human resource management and explain how managers plan for human resources.

2. Identify the steps involved in staffing a company.

3. Explain how organizations can develop workers' skills and manage workers who do not perform well.

4. Discuss the importance of wages, salaries, incentives, and benefits programs in attracting and keeping skilled workers.

5. Describe the legal and ethical issues involved in hiring, compensating, and managing workers.

6. Describe the major laws governing labor-management relations.

7. Identify the steps in the collective bargaining process.

DISCUSSION OF OPENING VIGNETTE

The narrative has been presented in a relatively unbiased fashion in an effort to lay the facts clearly on the table. However, a class discussion of Apple and Round Rock could easily lead to a bitter argument involving "conservatives" against "liberals." But the conservative-liberal debate has a strong monetary aspect to it, also. Traditionally, benefit programs covered single employees. They also covered married employees and their dependents. If we add to this traditional arrangement medical benefits (as an example) for the various categories of "partners" of <u>single</u> employees, then there is additional cost. Almost every person reading this case has already classified himself or herself as a liberal or conservative. An entrepreneur with generally liberal views might not be willing, however, to extend that liberalism to the company's cash drawer. A typical comment from such an entrepreneur might be: "It's fine with me for anyone to live with whomever they choose to live with--married or not, regardless of gender orientation. But don't ask <u>my company</u> to pay for it!" So far, we have not even touched the <u>moral</u> questions raised. These rather recent developments emphasize for us the fact that human resource managers must adapt to changing times. This is not saying that human resource managers must lose their sense of morality. However, if we again reach a time when there is keen competition by employers in the search for qualified employees, then outdated benefit programs may have to be changed in order to compete in the recruitment market. In addition, what might be termed "liberal" legislation of the future may require that these "partners" be added to the list of protected species--such as the handicapped, racial minorities, etc. Then there is the further matter of a company maintaining some degree of harmony with the people of the community. It is clear here that Apple and some city fathers of Round Rock do not see live-in partners in the same way. That's a bad way to start off a longstanding relationship. A company cannot be blind to the moral and ethical standards existing in the community outside the front gate of the plant.

1. When a gambling operation is considered for a community, there will be talk of "new revenues for the community" along with "moral decay and corruption." Draw some parallels between a gambling controversy and the Apple case at Round Rock.

2. What is your personal opinion on a benefits program considering live-in partners as "dependents" of single employees?

3. Is there indeed any reason for a firm to give consideration to the moral and ethical atmosphere of the community in which it plans to locate? Why or why not?

4. Some communities have welcomed with open arms large plants that soon began damaging the environment with their waste materials. Does such a situation in any way compare to the Apple controversy in Round Rock? Why or why not?

ANNOTATED KEY TERMS

Human resource management - The development and administration of programs to enhance the quality and performance of a company's workforce.

Job relatedness - The principle that all employment decisions should be based on the requirements of the jobs in question.

Person-job matching - The process of matching the right person to the right job.

Job analysis - An evaluation of the duties required by a job and the qualities required to perform it.

Job description - An outline of the objectives, tasks, and responsibilities of a job.

Job specification - A description of the skills, education, and experience required by a job.

Closed promotion system - A system by which managers decide, often informally, which workers are considered for promotion.

Open promotion system - A system by which employees apply, test, and interview for available jobs whose requirements are posted.

On-the-job training - Training, sometimes informal, conducted while an employee is at work.

Off-the-job training - Training conducted in a controlled environment away from the work site.

Vestibule training - Off-the-job training conducted in a simulated work environment.

Performance appraisal - An evaluation, often in writing, of an employee's job performance.

Disciplinary action - Action taken by management in response to employee behavior that is considered dangerous or disruptive.

Demotion - Action, such as removal to a lower position, taken by management in response to an employee's poor performance.

Separation (or termination) - The dismissal of an employee, usually for unacceptably poor performance.

Downsizing - The process of consolidating internal operations to make a firm more flexible and productive.

Compensation system - The total package offered by a company to employees in return for their labor.

<u>Wages</u> - Compensation in the form of money paid for time worked.

<u>Salary</u> - Compensation in the form of money paid for discharging the responsibilities of a job.

<u>Incentive program</u> - A special compensation program designed to motivate high performance.

<u>Merit salary system</u> - An incentive program linking increased compensation to performance in non-sales jobs.

<u>Profit-sharing plan</u> - An incentive program for distributing company profits above a certain level to employees.

<u>Gain-sharing plan</u> - An incentive plan for distributing bonuses to employees whose performances improve productivity.

<u>Pay-for-knowledge plan</u> - An incentive program to encourage employees to learn new skills or to become proficient at different jobs.

<u>Benefits</u> - Compensation other than wages or salaries.

<u>Workers' compensation insurance</u> - Legally required insurance for compensating workers injured on the job.

<u>Equal employment opportunity</u> - Legally mandated nondiscrimination in employment on the basis of race, color, creed, sex, or national origin.

<u>Affirmative action program</u> - A legally mandated program for recruiting qualified employees belonging to racial, gender, or ethnic groups that are underrepresented in an organization.

<u>Reverse discrimination</u> - The practice of discriminating against well-represented groups by overhiring members of underrepresented groups.

<u>Equal Pay Act of 1963</u> - A federal law forbidding different pay to men and women of equal experience performing work requiring equal skill, effort, and responsibility under similar conditions.

<u>Comparable worth</u> - The principle that women should receive the same pay for traditionally "female" jobs of the same worth to a company as traditionally "male" jobs.

<u>Occupational Safety and Health Administration (OSHA)</u> - The federal agency that sets and enforces guidelines for protecting workers from unsafe conditions and potential health hazards in the workplace.

<u>Employment at will</u> - The principle, increasingly modified by legislation and judicial decision, that organizations should be able to retain or dismiss employees at their discretion.

Workforce diversity - The range of workers' attitudes, values, and behaviors that differ by gender, race, and ethnicity.

Diversity training - Programs designed to improve employees' awareness of differences in co-workers' attitudes and behaviors.

Labor union - A group of individuals working together formally to achieve shared job-related goals.

Collective bargaining - The process by which labor and management negotiate conditions of employment for union-represented workers.

Norris-LaGuardia Act - A federal law (1932) that limited the ability of courts to issue injunctions prohibiting certain union activities.

Yellow-dog contract - An illegal contract clause requiring workers to begin and continue employment without union affiliation.

National Labor Relations Act (Wagner Act) - A federal law (1935) that protected the rights of workers to form unions, to bargain collectively, and to engage in strikes to achieve their goals.

National Labor Relations Board (NLRB) - A federal agency established by the National Labor Relations Act to enforce its provisions.

Fair Labor Standards Act - A federal law (1938) that set minimum wage and maximum number of hours in the work week.

Labor-Management Relations Act (Taft-Hartley Act) - A federal law (1947) that defined certain union practices as unfair and illegal.

Closed shop - A workplace, generally forbidden by the Taft-Hartley Act, in which an employer may hire only workers already belonging to a union.

Right-to-work laws - Statutes making it illegal to require union membership as a condition of employment.

Union shop - A workplace in which workers must join a union within a specified period after being hired.

Agency shop - A workplace in which workers must pay union dues even if they do not join.

Labor-Management Reporting and Disclosure Act (Landrum-Griffin Act) - A federal law (1959) that imposed regulations on internal union procedures, including elections of national leaders and filing of financial disclosure statements.

Bargaining unit - A designated group of employees who will be represented by a union.

Strike - A labor action in which employees temporarily walk off the job and refuse to work.

Economic strike - A strike usually triggered by a stalemate over one or more mandatory bargaining items.

Sympathy strike (or **secondary strike**) - A strike in which one union strikes to support action initiated by another union.

Wildcat strike - A strike that is unauthorized by the strikers' union.

Picketing - A labor action in which workers publicize their grievances at the entrance to an employer's facility.

Boycott - A labor action in which workers refuse to buy the products of a targeted employer.

Slowdown - A labor action in which workers perform jobs at a slower pace than normal.

Lockout - A management tactic whereby workers are denied access to the employer's workplace.

Strikebreaker - A worker hired as permanent or temporary replacement for a striking employee.

Mediation - A method of resolving a labor dispute in which a third party advises, but does not impose, a settlement.

Voluntary arbitration - A method of resolving a labor dispute in which both parties agree to submit to the judgment of a neutral party.

Compulsory arbitration - A method of resolving a labor dispute in which both parties are legally required to accept the judgment of a neutral party.

TRUE-FALSE QUESTIONS

1. Human resource specialists--sometimes called personnel managers--are employed by all firms.

2. Job analysis is an evaluation of the duties required by a particular job and the qualities required to perform it.

3. The first step in hiring new workers is to evaluate each individual and select the best candidate.

4. In a closed promotion system, managers decide which workers will be considered for promotions.

5. The posting of available jobs and their requirements is part of the closed promotion system.

6. The purpose of orientation is to help an employee learn the highly-specific aspects of the particular job he or she was hired to perform.

7. A salary is paid for time worked. For example, a worker who is paid by the hour is said to be receiving a salary.

8. A gain-sharing plan distributes bonuses to employees when a company's costs are reduced through greater work efficiency.

9. Reverse discrimination can occur when an organization concentrates so much on hiring from some minority groups that others are discriminated against.

10. In recent years, unions have been winning most certification elections.

MULTIPLE CHOICE QUESTIONS

1. It is an evaluation of the duties required by a particular job and the qualities required to perform it. What is it?

    a. job description
    b. job specification
    c. job analysis
    d. job posting

2. Which one of the following should be the first step in the hiring of new workers?

    a. select the best candidate
    b. on-site interviews
    c. evaluate each individual
    d. recruit a pool of applicants

113

3. Which one of the following is NOT a characteristic of a closed promotion system?

   a. details of job are posted
   b. popular especially in small firms
   c. managers decide who will be considered
   d. reliance on recommendations of immediate supervisors

4. Which one of the following is most likely to take place on a university campus?

   a. on-the-job training
   b. off-the-job training
   c. management development programs
   d. vestibule training programs

5. It involves consolidating internal operations to make them more flexible and productive. What is it?

   a. separation
   b. downsizing
   c. relocation
   d. maximizing

6. Some companies distribute bonuses to employees when a company's costs are reduced through greater work efficiency. What is the term used to designate such a program?

   a. profit sharing
   b. pay-for-knowledge
   c. gain sharing
   d. merit salary system

7. Women should receive the same wage for traditionally "female" jobs (such as secretary) as men do for traditional "male" jobs of the same worth to the company (for example, mechanic). What is the term that designates this concept?

   a. equal pay
   b. the "glass ceiling"
   c. gender bias
   d. comparable worth

8. At the Green Company, we note that an executive secretary with a bachelor's degree earns less money per year than a maintenance worker at Green with a high school diploma. This is a violation of which concept?

   a. equal pay
   b. the "glass ceiling"
   c. gender bias
   d. comparable worth

9. Mary Bascom has been a most effective middle manager for the Green Company for twelve years--longer service than any other middle manager with the firm. An opening in the "executive suite" has occurred and Mary has applied for it. She realizes she will not be seriously considered because she is a woman. This is best explained by which concept?

   a. equal pay
   b. the "glass ceiling"
   c. gender bias
   d. comparable worth

10. It is the process by which union leaders and managers negotiate common terms and conditions of employment for those workers represented by unions. What is it?

   a. collective bargaining
   b. certification
   c. givebacks
   d. decertification

11. Which act of Congress imposed severe limitations on the ability of the courts to issue injunctions prohibiting certain union activities, including strikes?

   a. Norris-LaGuardia Act
   b. Wagner Act
   c. Taft-Hartley Act
   d. Landrum-Griffin Act

12. Following World War II, a series of disruptive strikes turned much American public opinion against unions. Congress responded by passing the--

   a. Wagner Act
   b. Fair Labor Standards Act
   c. Taft-Hartley Act
   d. Landrum-Griffin Act

13. Which one of the following Congressional actions imposes regulations on internal union procedures?

   a. Wagner Act
   b. Fair Labor Standards Act
   c. Taft-Hartley Act
   d. Landrum-Griffin Act

14. It is defined as a method of resolving a labor dispute in which a third party advises, but does not impose, a settlement. What is it?

   a. compulsory arbitration
   b. mediation
   c. voluntary arbitration
   d. anti-lockout

15. The textbook tells us that a lockout was used (without success) by a prominent group in 1990. Identify that group.

    a. baseball team owners
    b. General Motors board of directors
    c. General Mills board of directors
    d. an airlines management group

16. Which of the following is a management tactic to be resorted to in the event of an impasse?

    a. boycott
    b. sympathy strike
    c. lockout
    d. picketing

17. Which of the following is capable of dictating a settlement to a labor-management dispute?

    a. negotiation
    b. mediation
    c. certification
    d. arbitration

18. A union demand for veto power over the promotion of managerial personnel would be classified as a--

    a. dream situation
    b. permissive bargaining item
    c. normal occurrence in industry
    d. basis for a lockout

19. Which one of the following tactics utilized by workers is least likely to have the blessing of the workers' union?

    a. sympathy strike
    b. wildcat strike
    c. slowdown
    d. honoring another union's picket line

20. Which of the following is a union tactic to be resorted to in the event of an impasse?

    a. boycott
    b. lockout
    c. strikebreaker
    d. permanent replacement

WRITING TO LEARN

1. List and explain all the steps involved for the human resources staff from the moment a position at a firm is vacant to the moment that a replacement has been hired.

2. The Opening Vignette mentioned some aspects of human resources management that did not have to be considered some thirty years ago. Identify some other changes in human resources matters that have occurred over the past thirty years.

3. List, explain and give examples of the various incentive programs treated in the textbook. Which one do you think is the most effective? Why?

4. Completely explain the issues related to and the controversy surrounding employment at will. At what point do you feel the courts have interfered--if at all--in an entrepreneur's right to run his or her own business?

5. List and explain the steps that can lead to a person being separated or terminated. Under the plan you explain, what opportunity does the employee have to change his or her way of behaving?

6. Show the differences between the Wagner Act of 1935 and the Taft-Hartley Act of 1947. Which is the more friendly to the union labor movement?

7. Write of that which was accomplished by the passage of the Norris-LaGuardia Act.

8. Expound upon the weapons available to management in its contest with labor unions in the event that an impasse occurs. For one of these weapons, develop a narrative explaining how such a maneuver can be implemented.

9. Tell how a labor union on strike might go about organizing a boycott against the firm where the strike is taking place.

DISCUSSION OF BUSINESS CASE 9

Perhaps ever since the founding of the United States, there has been debate over just how much the government should involve itself in the affairs of individual businesses. Everyone agrees that there must be some government regulation of business. Where we disagree is on the matter of how much government involvement in business we want. The survey by The Wall Street Journal looking into how African-Americans are doing with American firms brings out another aspect of government getting involved in business enterprises. Even though legislation is passed, and even though affirmative action guidelines and programs are developed and implemented, and even though many employers want to comply with their responsibility to give African-Americans an equal opportunity, still we see, according to the Journal, that something about the practical application of the concept is not working! There will always be ways to explain away the fact that jobs for African-Americans are dwindling. First, it can be said that there are not enough qualified African-American candidates for the jobs that are opening up at relatively high levels in the organization. Then, we can say that many of the service jobs that seemed to match the training of some African-American workers are disappearing from the scene. Another explanation is that many companies that would be willing to hire African-Americans are located in areas where there are none. It seems that large groups of African-Americans are falling between the cracks. It all sounds a little like the story of movie star Clark Gable during World War II. (Ask your parents and their parents if they remember Clark Gable! They will.) Gable, who was no youngster at the time, enlisted in the Army Air Corps (forerunner of the U.S. Air Force) and went through officer training. He flew a few missions in bombers over Europe. Then, suddenly, the Army Air Corps released Clark Gable and sent him home! Their explanation was: "He is too old for combat, yet he is too inexperienced for command." Similarly, to many African-Americans corporations seem to be saying: "You are over-qualified for the jobs we have, or you are under-qualified, you live in an area where we are not adding personnel, your skills do not match our needs, etc." Nevertheless, additional efforts must be made to see that bad economic times do not always hit African-Americans the hardest.

1. Why is employment of African-Americans dropping while figures for Hispanics and Asians are going up?

2. If it were known that many of the Hispanics and Asians involved in this survey are not yet American citizens, should this make a difference in their being hired over African-Americans who are U.S. citizens? Why or why not?

3. In considering minority employees, is it important that the federal government know which minorities are represented? Why?

4. Evaluate this statement: "Racial prejudice has been virtually eliminated from human resources recruitment."

ANSWERS TO TRUE-FALSE QUESTIONS

1. F (p. 205)
2. T (p. 206)
3. F (p. 207)
4. T (p. 210)
5. F (p. 210)
6. F (p. 210)
7. F (p. 213-214)
8. T (p. 216)
9. T (p. 217)
10. F (p. 219)

ANSWERS TO MULTIPLE CHOICE QUESTIONS

1. c (p. 206)
2. d (p. 207-209)
3. a (p. 210)
4. c (p. 210-211)
5. b (p. 212)
6. c (p. 216)
7. d (p. 217)
8. d (p. 217)
9. b (p. 217)
10. a (p. 219)
11. a (p. 220-221)
12. c (p. 221)
13. d (p. 222)
14. b (p. 225)
15. a (p. 225)
16. c (p. 225)
17. d (p. 225)
18. b (p. 223)
19. b (p. 224)
20. a (p. 224-225)

CHAPTER TEN

PRODUCING GOODS AND SERVICES

CHAPTER OVERVIEW

Utility--time, place, ownership, and form--is the ability of a product to satisfy a human want. While goods are produced, services are performed and are characterized by intangibility, customization, and unstorability. An operations process is the set of methods and technologies used in the production of a good or service. Production processes can be classified by: type of transformation technology; analytic or synthetic nature of the process; pattern of product flow; and extent of customer contact. Managers develop a firm's long-range production through forecasts. Planning and forecasting activities may be classified into the categories of capacity, location, layout, quality, and methods planning. A master production schedule shows which products will be produced, when production will occur, and what resources will be used during the scheduled time period. PERT is useful in managing customized projects whose success means coordinating numerous activities. Materials management involves not just controlling but also planning and organizing the flow of materials. Both just-in-time (JIT) and material requirements planning (MRP) seek to bring together all needed materials and parts at the precise moment that they are required for each production stage. In their battle for competitiveness, U.S. firms are turning to mechanization, automation, and computerization.

LEARNING OBJECTIVES

1. Identify the characteristics that distinguish service operations from goods production.

2. Describe the factors involved in operations planning and scheduling.

3. Explain the activities involved in production control, including materials management and the use of production control tools, and describe the special production control problems of service operations.

4. Characterize the kinds of automation currently in use in production operations.

5. Explain the advantages and risks of small versus large production companies.

DISCUSSION OF OPENING VIGNETTE

The saga of Dell, Compaq, and Gateway 2000 is a familiar tale that tells us several things about operating a business in a competitive world. The first lesson is that it is very difficult to maintain a given level of quality in services. Nevertheless, this level of quality must be maintained if the firm is to continue to be successful! Similar to the Dell story is that of an auto repair shop we shall call Charlie's. Charlie Jones and his brother Mark opened an automotive repair business. They were highly-capable mechanics with many years of experience and pleasing personalities. When a customer came to Charlie's early in the morning, the brothers quickly diagnosed the car problem and had it satisfactorily remedied by noon the same day-- regardless of how major the repair may have been. As a result, word spread throughout the community that Charlie's was the place to go for car repair. Day after day, Charlie's created more and more satisfied customers. The business grew. Mark and Charlie had to add two or three other mechanics to their operation to handle all the business flowing in. Of course, the new employees weren't as sharp as the original brothers, and the volume of customers was getting hard to handle. Now at Charlie's, you take your car in at 7:00 A.M. on a Monday and it may be ready for you by Tuesday night at 6:00 P.M. Charlie has been known to whine: "Oh heck, I'll just open a brand-new one-stall shop and take in only two cars per day. That way I can retain my high standards of quality." Charlie's and Dell both need to adapt to increasing volume. The second lesson is revealed by the fact that just down the street from Charlie's, Lake Blaine Automotive opened and provides the same service but adds: free breakfast while you wait, pick up and delivery of your car, and a free car wash. Many of Charlie's customers are now flocking to Lake Blaine Automotive. Yes, competition has set in, and Charlie's must react with some special services of his own. At this moment, Dell finds itself in Charlie's shoes. What will they do?

1. Based on the narratives on Dell and Charlie's, what do you recommend that Dell and Charlie do to win back sales that may be going to competitors?

2. Explain just how important you feel prompt delivery seems to be in the personal computer industry.

3. If Dell's products were of slightly better quality than those of Gateway 2000 and Compaq, could Dell worry less about its promptness of delivery? Why or why not?

4. The old saying goes: "Build a better mousetrap and the world will beat a path to your door...." In light of what you now know of Dell, finish that sentence by starting with the word "however."

ANNOTATED KEY TERMS

Service operations - Business activities that provide tangible and intangible services.

Goods production - Business activities that create tangible products.

Utility - A product's ability to satisfy a human want.

Operations (or production) management - Systematic direction and control of the processes that transform resources into finished products.

Operations process - A set of methods and technologies used in the production of a good or service.

Analytic process - A production process in which resources are broken down into components to create finished products.

Synthetic process - A production process in which resources are combined to create finished products.

Continuous process - A production process in which a product moves through a plant in a continuous, straightforward manner.

Intermittent (or job-shop) process - A production process in which a product moves through plant equipment and/or departments in a series of stages.

Routing - A unique set of steps required to produce a product.

High-contact system - Level of service-customer contact in which the customer receives the service as part of the system.

Low-contact system - Level of service-customer contact in which the customer need not be a part of the system to receive the service.

Forecast - Facet of a long-range production plan that predicts future demand.

Capacity - Amount of a product that a company can produce under normal working conditions.

Process layout - Spatial arrangement of production activities that groups equipment and people according to function.

Product layout - Spatial arrangement of production activities designed to move resources through a smooth, fixed sequence of steps.

Assembly line - Product layout in which a product moves step by step through a plant on conveyer belts or other equipment until it is completed.

Fixed-position layout - Product layout in which production activities--labor, materials, and equipment--are taken to the location where the work is done.

Master production schedule - Schedule showing which products will be produced, when production will take place, and what resources will be used.

Gantt chart - Production schedule diagramming the steps in a project and specifying the time required for each.

PERT chart - Production schedule specifying the sequence and critical path for performing the steps in a project.

Production control - Process of monitoring production performance by comparing results with plans.

Follow-up - Production-control activity for ensuring that production decisions are being implemented.

Materials management - Planning, organizing, and controlling the flow of materials from design through distribution of finished goods.

Standardization - Use, where possible, of standard and uniform components in the production process.

Inventory control - In materials management, the receiving, storing, handling, and counting of all raw materials, partly finished goods, and finished goods.

Holding costs - Costs of keeping extra supplies or inventory on hand.

Supplier selection - Process of finding and selecting suppliers from whom to buy.

Just-in-time production system (JIT) - Production method that brings all materials and parts needed at each production stage at the precise moment they are required.

Material requirements planning (MRP) - Production-control method in which a bill of materials is used to ensure that the right amounts of materials are delivered to the right place at the right time.

Bill of materials - Production-control tool that specifies the necessary ingredients (raw materials and components) of a product, the order in which they should be combined, and how many of each are needed to make one "batch."

Manufacturing resource planning (MRP II) - Advanced version of MRP that ties together all parts of an organization into its production activities.

__Quality control__ - Management of the production process designed to manufacture goods or supply services that meet specific quality standards.

__Mechanization__ - Process of using machines to do work previously done by people.

__Automation__ - Process of performing production operations with either minimal or no human involvement.

__Robotics__ - Construction, maintenance, and use of computer-controlled machines in manufacturing operations.

__Computer-integrated manufacturing (CIM)__ - Computer system which drives robots and controls the materials and supplies flows and which can also manage material requirements planning and just-in-time production systems.

__Computer-aided design (CAD)__ - Computer analysis that allows designers to simulate conditions and test design performance.

__Computer-aided manufacturing (CAM)__ - Computer system used to design and control equipment needed in the manufacturing process.

__Decision support system (DSS)__ - Management information system giving users access to both decision models and data needed to make decisions.

TRUE-FALSE QUESTIONS

1. When a department store opens its "Trim-a-Tree" department in the fall, it creates time utility.

2. Services like rubbish collection, transportation, child care and house cleaning cannot be produced ahead of time and then stored.

3. An important value in services is the intangible value that the customer experiences in the form of pleasure, satisfaction, or a feeling of safety.

4. The old notion that services cannot be stored has largely been discredited today.

5. As a service to customers, the Bay Area Rapid Transit System (BART) is a high-contact system.

6. In a process layout, equipment and people are grouped together according to function.

7. Production control requires managers to monitor production performance, in part by comparing results with detailed plans and schedules.

8. A negative aspect of a just-in-time (JIT) system is that it leads to excessive inventory costs.

9. The textbook indicates that mechanization is a natural extension of automation.

10. Although Japanese companies pioneered their use, U.S. firms are becoming increasingly interested in robotics.

MULTIPLE CHOICE QUESTIONS

1. When a manufacturing firm turns raw materials into finished goods, that manufacturing firm is creating which kind of utility?

    a. time
    b. place
    c. ownership or possession
    d. form

2. A wholesaler is able to deliver balls and bats to retailers well in advance of the baseball-softball season. That wholesaler has thus created which kind of utility?

    a. time
    b. place
    c. ownership or possession
    d. form

3. "I buy it, take it home, use it, and enjoy it. It gives me a warm cuddly feeling." This statement captures the meaning of which kind of utility?

    a. time
    b. place
    c. ownership or possession
    d. form

4. We can say that services, like fresh fruit, can be perishable. This statement relates to which of the following qualities of services listed by the textbook?

    a. unstorability
    b. intangibility
    c. customization
    d. high customer contact

5. Airline flight 877 from Boston to New York on May 7, 1999, in seat 11-C can be taken only once. This fact relates to which one of the following characteristics of services?

    a. unstorability
    b. intangibility
    c. customization
    d. high customer contact

6. From the list below, select the firm that put a price freeze on plywood after Hurricane Andrew hit Homestead, Florida.

    a. Homestead Lumber Yard
    b. South Florida Supply
    c. Home Depot
    d. Home Supply and Materials, Ltd.

7. When you visit a physician, you expect to be examined for your symptoms. This expectation relates to which of the following?

    a. unstorability
    b. medical close touch
    c. renticular bicaterization
    d. customization

8. Select below a characteristic that should be possessed by a local gas company employee making service calls that is not necessary for a gas pipe installer working for a mobile home manufacturer.

    a. skill at repairing damaged pipes
    b. interpersonal skills
    c. knowledge of natural gas functioning
    d. safety techniques

9. Which one of the following is most likely to be considered a high-contact system?

    a. lawn care
    b. barber
    c. electric utilities
    d. auto repair

10. Which one of the following is most likely to be considered a low-contact system?

    a. doctor
    b. airlines
    c. car rental
    d. trash collection

11. Which one of the following is most likely to be considered a high-contact system?

    a. dentist
    b. banking by mail
    c. mail delivery
    d. television

12. Which one of the following is NOT one of the major categories of planning and forecasting provided by the textbook?

    a. capacity
    b. location
    c. layout
    d. financial

13. Which one of the following is the best example of a process layout in action?

    a. food processing
    b. bakery
    c. computer assembly
    d. automobile assembly line

14. Which one of the following is the best example of a product layout in action?

    a. job shop
    b. dry cleaning shop
    c. assembly line
    d. machine shop

15. Which of the following is NOT a major area of materials management?

    a. purchasing
    b. warehousing
    c. transportation
    d. shaping

16. For many years, purchasing departments routinely purchased quantities of materials large enough to fill their needs for long periods of time. This practice is called--

    a. forward buying
    b. stock in trade
    c. hunking
    d. full stocking

17. Which of the following is least likely to be considered a holding cost?

    a. opportunity
    b. ordering
    c. insurance
    d. storage

18. It specifies the necessary ingredients, the order in which they should be combined, and the quantity of each ingredient needed to make one "batch" of the product. What is it?

    a. master PERT chart
    b. bill of materials
    c. just-in-time
    d. quality circle

19. What is the specific term that the textbook has assigned to the performing of operations with either minimal or no human involvement?

    a. automation
    b. mechanization
    c. robotics
    d. neural networks

20. There are 20,000 robots in use now in the United States. How many are in use in Japan?

    a. 20,000
    b. 40,000
    c. 80,000
    d. 121,000

WRITING TO LEARN

1. Define and give several examples of each of the four major kinds of utility.

2. Using airlines, motion picture theaters, and hotels as examples, explain why the textbook indicates that services are "unstorable."

3. Explain the intangibility of services. Try to fit a college education into your explanation.

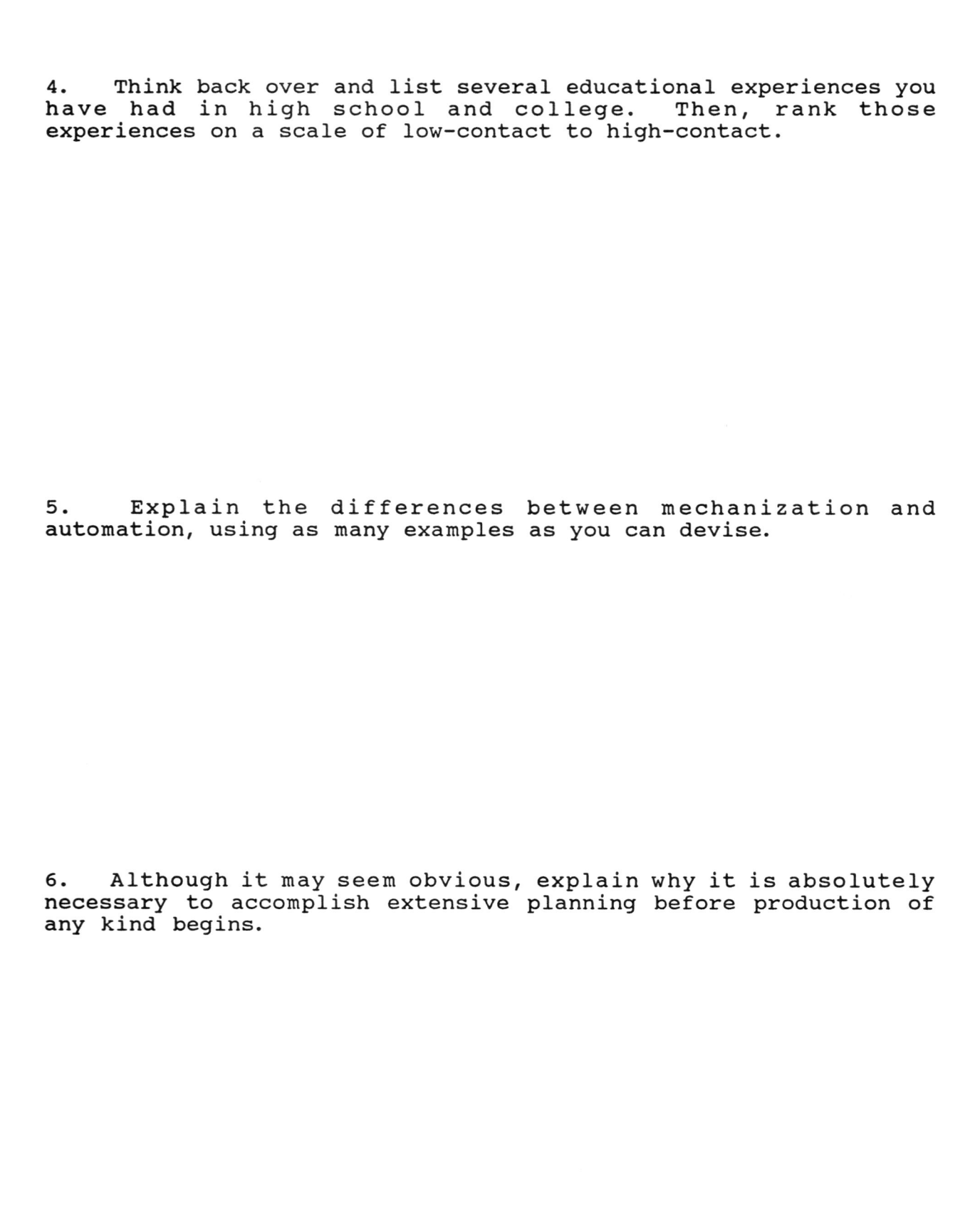

4. Think back over and list several educational experiences you have had in high school and college. Then, rank those experiences on a scale of low-contact to high-contact.

5. Explain the differences between mechanization and automation, using as many examples as you can devise.

6. Although it may seem obvious, explain why it is absolutely necessary to accomplish extensive planning before production of any kind begins.

7. Without getting involved in definitions, provide as many illustrations as you can of the two major layouts--process and product.

8. No doubt about it, in theory just-in-time (JIT) production systems make good sense. Your assignment now, however, is to give some reasons from the real world why JIT will run into difficulties.

9. You are helping the author of a textbook on modern production techniques. You have been asked to explain CAD/CAM. Good luck!

DISCUSSION OF BUSINESS CASE 10

"When things are going along so well, why do we have to hit a snag like this?" That's a question that Allied Automotive executives could well have been asking one another after discovering that selling brake pads to Toyota was going to be a major headache. But the Toyota hurdle is typical of challenges that businesses face regularly. One approach by Allied Automotive might well have been to conclude: "The extra effort involved in making Toyota happy will not result in sufficient rewards. Let's terminate our relationship with Toyota and go on to servicing other less picky clients." Such an approach would have been very sensible and very good for Allied--in the <u>short term</u>. However, Allied executives concluded that the Toyota relationship--if it could ever be firmly established--could bring in massive new revenues at some point in the distant future. Allied Automotive, then, decided to go after benefits in the <u>long term</u>. You will note that to do this, the company was taking a big backward step. But that one backward step has enabled the firm to take TWO steps <u>forward</u>! The fact that you are in college right now shows that you understand the benefits of taking a backward step in order to take two steps forward. You may have high school friends who right now are working and making a respectable income. As for you, you've taken a step backward financially in order to go to college. But when you obtain that bachelor's degree, you'll be taking two steps forward. The Allied Automotive decision also tells us something about the need that any business has for a strong financial base. In large manufacturing corporations this strength is often expressed through commitments to research and development (R&D). While Allied Automotive was making all the necessary painful adjustments to suit Toyota, there was no revenue coming in from Toyota. But Allied was stable enough to withstand this treading of water. Many small sole proprietorships would be incapable of making such huge adjustments in the absence of new revenues from a Toyota. Allied was able to hang on, and is now very glad that it did.

1. Was Toyota unrealistic in its demands on Allied? Why or why not?

2. Give all the reasons you can why Allied could well have elected to cease relationships with Toyota.

3. Often, people will say: "You're a better person because of what happened." Apply this expression to Allied Automotive following its Toyota ordeal.

4. With Allied and Toyota in mind, explain the constant competition between short-term and long-term goals.

ANSWERS TO TRUE-FALSE- QUESTIONS

1.	F (p. 236)	6.	T (p. 244)
2.	T (p. 238)	7.	T (p. 246)
3.	T (p. 238)	8.	F (p. 248)
4.	F (p. 238)	9.	F (p. 250)
5.	T (p. 239)	10.	T (p. 251)

ANSWERS TO MULTIPLE CHOICE QUESTIONS

1.	d (p. 236)	11.	a (p. 239)
2.	a (p. 236)	12.	d (p. 242)
3.	c (p. 236)	13.	b (p. 244)
4.	a (p. 238)	14.	c (p. 244)
5.	a (p. 238)	15.	d (p. 247)
6.	c (p. 240)	16.	a (p. 247)
7.	d (p. 238)	17.	b (p. 247)
8.	b (p. 238)	18.	b (p. 248)
9.	b (p. 239)	19.	a (p. 250)
10.	d (p. 239)	20.	c (p. 251)

CHAPTER ELEVEN

INCREASING PRODUCTIVITY AND QUALITY

CHAPTER OVERVIEW

Productivity is a measure of economic performance. It compares how much we produce with the resources we use to produce it. Quality means fitness for use--offering features that consumers want. Despite the much publicized "productivity crisis," the United States remains the most productive nation in the world, but our productivity is not increasing as fast as it did in the past. Value-added analysis is the evaluation of all work activities, materials flows, and paperwork to determine the value that they add for customers. Gross domestic product (GDP) is the value of all goods and services produced in the economy, excluding foreign earnings and income. Total quality management (TQM) includes any activity necessary for getting quality goods and services into the marketplace. TQM involves planning, organizing, leading, and controlling. Statistical process control (SPC) refers to methods by which managers can analyze variations in production data. Quality/cost studies are useful because they not only identify a firm's current costs but also reveal areas with the largest cost-savings potential. One proven tool for improving quality is the use of quality improvement teams, sometimes called quality circles. By continuous improvement is meant the ongoing commitment to improving products and processes, step by step, in pursuit of ever-increasing customer satisfaction.

LEARNING OBJECTIVES

1. Describe the connection between productivity and quality.

2. Explain the decline in U.S. productivity and why some observers consider it a crisis.

3. Explain total and partial measures of productivity and show how they are used to keep track of national, industry-wide, and company-wide productivity.

4. Identify the activities involved in total quality management and describe four tools that companies can use to achieve it.

5. List six ways in which companies can compete by improving productivity and quality.

DISCUSSION OF OPENING VIGNETTE

Somewhat like an embattled family in a television soap opera, Jaguar was facing an impressive list of problems. Here's a quick recap. Corporate culture that stifled initiative, inefficient manufacturing system, unrealistic annual net income expectations, bitter labor-management relations, restrictive union practices, and aging production facilities, not to mention a growing international reputation for shoddy workmanship. Although this is the chapter on productivity and quality, there is the excellent possibility that many of the problems at Jaguar stemmed from faulty leadership, absence of motivation, abysmal morale, and haphazard human resources practices--matters covered in earlier chapters. Notice that workforce cooperation with management increased simultaneously with a cutting of the force from 12,000 to 6,500 persons. This may be telling us that among the 6,500 who were lucky enough to keep their jobs there was a feeling of gratitude at having a job. Such gratitude can often translate into a more conscientious approach to one's work. Just how much connection is there between human relations and product quality? The finest quality procedures in the world will achieve very little if the human resources do not implement them. Perhaps in high school, you were required to read The Jungle by Upton Sinclair. It is about the terrible conditions in which packinghouse employees worked in Chicago around 1900. Sinclair tells of the dangers there and of the lack of purity and cleanliness in the preparation of meat products. Although Sinclair's mission was to expose the unenlightened harshness of the managerial spirit in those plants, Sinclair could not help but reveal that the workers were totally apathetic. He indicated that workers would knowingly and uncaringly allow rat excrement--and indeed rats themselves--to go into sausage that was shipped out across America. Obviously, to state it in most subtle fashion, such workers had no sense of quality control. Hopefully, for the future, conditions will be better at Jaguar.

1. Explain what relationship you see between the workers at the old Jaguar plant and the workers in The Jungle of Sinclair.

2. Evaluate this statement: "As far as I'm concerned, Jaguar should have shut down its operations for five years, then opened again on a totally new basis."

3. Considering the number of parts that went into each Jaguar, do you feel that the firm was trying to attain a level of sophistication that was unrealistically high? Why or why not?

4. Explain the possible importance of a "new spirit of labor-management cooperation" at Jaguar.

ANNOTATED KEY TERMS

<u>Quality</u> - A product's fitness for use; its success in offering features that consumers want.

<u>Level of productivity</u> - Dollar value of goods and services relative to the resources used to produce them.

<u>Growth rate of productivity</u> - Annual increase in a nation's output over the previous year.

<u>Value-added analysis</u> - Process of evaluating all work activities, materials flows, and paperwork to determine the value they add for customers.

<u>Total-factor productivity ratio</u> - Productivity measure that considers all types of input resources--labor, capital, materials, energy, and purchased business services.

<u>Partial productivity ratio</u> - Productivity measure that considers only certain input sources.

<u>Materials productivity</u> - Partial productivity ratio calculated by dividing the total outputs by total materials inputs.

<u>Labor productivity</u> - Partial productivity ratio calculated by dividing total outputs by total labor inputs.

<u>Gross domestic product (GDP)</u> - The value of all goods and services produced by a nation's economy, excluding foreign earnings and income.

<u>Total quality management (TQM) (or quality assurance)</u> - The sum of all activities involved in getting quality products into the marketplace.

<u>Performance quality</u> - The performance features offered by a product.

<u>Quality reliability</u> - Consistency of a product's quality from unit to unit.

<u>Competitive product analysis</u> - Process by which a company analyzes a competitor's products to determine desirable improvements in its own.

<u>Statistical process control (SPC)</u> - Evaluation methods that allow managers to analyze variations in a company's production data.

<u>Process variation</u> - Variation in products arising from changes in production inputs.

<u>Process capability study</u> - Process control method that measures product samples to determine the amount of total process variation.

Specification limits - Boundaries of acceptable quality in the production of a good or service.

Control chart - Process control method that plots test-sampling results on a diagram to determine when a process is beginning to depart from normal operating conditions.

Control limit - Critical value on a control chart indicating the level at which quality deviation is sufficiently unacceptable and merits investigation.

Quality/cost study - Method of improving quality by identifying current costs and areas with the greatest cost-saving potential.

Internal failures - Reducible costs incurred during production and before bad products leave a plant.

External failures - Reducible costs incurred after defective products have left a plant.

Quality improvement team (or quality circle) - TQM team in which groups of employees work together as a team to improve quality.

Benchmarking - Process by which a company implements the best practices of other companies to improve its own products.

Continuous improvement - A firm's ongoing commitment to improving products and processes, step by step, in the pursuit of ever-increasing customer satisfaction.

Employee empowerment - Concept that all employees are valuable contributors to a firm's business and should be entrusted with certain decisions regarding their work.

TRUE-FALSE QUESTIONS

1. Despite the much publicized "productivity crisis," the United States remains the most productive nation in the world.

2. The growth rate of productivity is the annual increase in a nation's output over the previous year.

3. In the United States, during our present "productivity crisis," productivity is no longer increasing from year to year.

4. If current growth rates continue, per capita productivity in both France and Italy will surpass that of the United States sometime before the year 2000.

5. Productivity is a measure of economic performance: It compares how much we produce with the resources we use to produce it.

6. High productivity gives a company a competitive edge although its costs are higher.

7. Outputs are the resources used to create inputs.

8. Gross domestic product is the new term meaning the same thing as gross national product.

9. Japan's highest honor for industrial achievement is called the Deming Award for Quality.

10. Competitive product analysis refers to methods by which managers can analyze variations in production data.

MULTIPLE CHOICE QUESTIONS

1. It is the annual increase in a nation's output over the previous year. What is it?

   a. gross domestic product
   b. gross national product
   c. growth rate of productivity
   d. value-added analysis

2. Which one of the following is defined as the evaluation of all work activities, materials flows, and paperwork to determine the value they add for customers?

   a. gross domestic product
   b. gross national product
   c. growth rate of productivity
   d. value-added analysis

3. Which one of the following best describes how to calculate labor productivity?

    a. hours worked times hourly rate
    b. outputs divided by labor inputs
    c. labor inputs divided by total output
    d. total labor wages divided by gross domestic product

4. Which one of the following best describes how to calculate materials productivity?

    a. total materials costs per unit times expected outputs
    b. outputs divided by materials
    c. materials divided by outputs
    d. value-added quotient plus cost of acquiring materials

5. Which one of the following best describes how to calculate labor productivity of a country or national labor productivity ratio?

    a. gross domestic product divided by total number of workers
    b. gross national product divided by total number of workers
    c. average wage of workers times number of units produced
    d. gross domestic product times average wage of workers

6. Which response below best relates to the saga of W. Edwards Deming?

    a. reluctant and limited acceptance by the Japanese
    b. not honored in his homeland
    c. employee of Florida Power and Light Company
    d. first proponent of value-added analysis

7. It is defined as including any activity necessary for getting quality goods and services into the marketplace. What is it?

    a. performance quality
    b. production
    c. total quality management
    d. quality circles

8. What term have we given to the idea that quality belongs to each person who creates it while performing a job?

    a. total quality management
    b. quality reliability
    c. quality ownership
    d. product quality standards

9. Which one of the following is the best illustration of competitive product analysis?

   a. tearing down a competitor's dishwasher, part by part
   b. analyzing competitor's quality-assurance techniques
   c. government ranking of various products' quality levels
   d. friendly quality competition among teams within a plant

10. As employees, materials, work methods, and equipment change, so will production outputs. These variations are called--

   a. quality deviations
   b. quality ownership
   c. production variations
   d. process variations

11. There are at many plants groups of employees who work in units to improve both their work methods and the products they make. They meet on company time in the company's facility. We usually refer to them as--

   a. product process professionals
   b. production teams
   c. trouble-shooters
   d. quality circles

12. To improve its own products and services, one company finds and implements the best practices of other companies. We call this practice--

   a. competitive product analysis
   b. benchmarking
   c. comparative quality circles
   c. copycat coving

13. Which firm, a winner of the prestigious Malcolm Baldridge National Quality Award and mentioned in the textbook, uses interactive video to train and test all 45,000 employees who have direct contact with the company's customers?

   a. Procter & Gamble
   b. AT&T
   c. Federal Express
   d. American Express

14. Which firm has its employees, in their free moments at work, call longstanding customers to thank them for their patronage and to ask for suggestions for improvements in service?

   a. First Hawaiian Bank
   b. Federal Express
   c. AT&T
   d. Procter & Gamble

15. Which phrase below best describes the United States in its efforts at factory automation during the 1980's and 1990's?

    a. world leader
    b. lagging behind Western Europe and Japan
    c. ahead of Western Europe but behind Japan
    d. ahead of Japan but behind Western Europe

16. "Six-sigma quality" translates into how many manufacturing defects?

    a. three per million
    b. ten per million
    c. seventy-five per million
    d. ninety-five per million

17. Motorola is a good example of a firm trying to upgrade its quality. Company officials say that by the year 2001 their quality will have reached the level of--

    a. three defects per million
    b. two defects per million
    c. one defect per million
    d. one defect per billion

18. Motorola is a good example of a firm that, instead of emphasizing short-term results, has an ongoing commitment to improving products and processes, step by step, in pursuit of ever-increasing customer satisfaction. We call this approach--

    a. continuous improvement
    b. quality circles
    c. Quality 2001
    d. internal defects

19. What do we call the principle that all employees are valuable contributors to a business and should be entrusted with certain decisions regarding their work?

    a. management teams from below (MTFB)
    b. quality circles
    c. employee empowerment
    d. strength through growth

20. One company in the late 1980's invested $8,000 per employee in training programs. With better-trained employees, the company has been able to reduce its number of managers and rely more heavily on a team approach to solving problems. Name that company.

    a. Federal Express
    b. Sweetheart Cup Company
    c. Wallace Company
    d. Melroy Lamps

WRITING TO LEARN

1. Keeping in mind that quality in manufacturing a product costs money, develop a narrative in which you weigh the positive aspects of fine quality against the negative aspects of additional costs to the organization.

2. If blame can be assessed, assign fault for the fact that American productivity growth from year to year is decreasing.

3. Explain the major advantages of value-added analysis. Looking at the value-added analysis factor called "paperwork," explain how monetary gains or losses may be hard to determine.

4. Explain how total quality management (TQM) could be implemented in a non-manufacturing setting, such as a hospital or advertising agency.

5. Let us say that a new firm has a new approach to product quality control. Each worker will inspect his or her own work. Tell why this will or will not be effective.

6. The most complete way to check the quality of a firm's products is to carefully inspect each and every item manufactured. This is too cumbersome. So, a check through statistical samples is done. Explain why the latter approach would be especially necessary in an ammunition plant!

7. Explain employee empowerment and tell all the reasons for its improving of the work environment. Tell of dangers in the concept if some managers (where it is being implemented) do not really believe in it.

8. What do you think of Motorola's plan to have quality at the level of 1 defect per billion by the year 2001. Is this a realistic expectation or merely a public relations ploy?

9. Explain what happens in benchmarking and in competitive product analysis. With this in mind, explain why in war time, Side 1 is overjoyed when a Side 2 aircraft is shot down over Side 1's territory, and that aircraft experiences virtually no damage in the process.

DISCUSSION OF BUSINESS CASE 11

Here's a quoted clause from the case narrative: "Employees often acted as if the customer didn't matter." We hate to tell you, but that clause does not describe a new or rare phenomenon. Successful companies are those that can eliminate such a don't-care attitude on the part of their employees. And we can see that IBM Credit Corporation in those early days was a role model of inefficiency and a gathering hive for Theory X employees. Like IBM Credit, many firms and government agencies will warn: "Allow six weeks for processing." A true statement of the situation should be: "Allow 30 minutes for processing and an additional six weeks for your paperwork to lay on someone's desk unattended." Workers in such large offices often confirm that Theory X managers are right (see Chapter Eight); some people are just lazy! A few minutes with a man we shall call Ned Brown illustrates the point. Ned had to go to a large federal agency to handle a claim. He told the receptionist that he wanted Mrs. Whitney to handle his problem. The receptionist told him: "Your name is Brown, and Mrs. Whitney handles only those people whose names start with L through Z. We can arrange it, but you'll have to wait a long time." Ned Brown then explained his interest in Mrs. Whitney: "I'll be delighted to wait for Mrs. Whitney, and that is because she is the only person among all you people [Ned actually said "turkeys"] who knows what she's doing. The last time I came in they assigned me to Mr. Flinch--there he is over there--and he didn't know Government Form A from a Beatles poster. And the last thing on his mind was trying to help me. Yes, I'll gladly wait for Mrs. Whitney." Thankfully, at IBM Credit Corporation, the entire system was "reengineered," and there are clear hints that the number of personnel involved has been reduced. It would be hoped that in the reengineering process, workers like Mr. Flinch would be reassigned to a setting where their true talents can successfully bloom.

1. Expand upon the comment above that actual processing takes only 30 minutes while the six weeks is for your form to lay unattended on someone's desk.

2. You call an organization like the IBM Credit Corporation (before it was reengineered). How do you react when for several minutes you find yourself being addressed by a <u>recording</u>?

3. Tell why it seems almost mandatory that making minor changes in IBM Credit would not be effective, and why the entire organization had to be torn down brick by brick and reassembled from scratch.

4. Think back to some business institution where you have worked. How would you go about reengineering that organization?

ANSWERS TO TRUE-FALSE QUESTIONS

1. T (p. 262)
2. T (p. 263)
3. F (p. 263)
4. T (p. 263)
5. T (p. 261)

6. F (p. 264)
7. F (p. 265)
8. F (p. 266)
9. T (p. 267)
10. F (p. 269)

ANSWERS TO MULTIPLE CHOICE QUESTIONS

1. c (p. 263)
2. d (p. 265)
3. b (p. 266)
4. b (p. 266)
5. a (p. 266)
6. b (p. 267)
7. c (p. 267)
8. c (p. 269)
9. a (p. 269)
10. d (p. 270-271)

11. d (p. 274)
12. b (p. 276)
13. c (p. 276-277)
14. a (p. 276-277)
15. b (p. 277)
16. a (p. 277)
17. d (p. 277-278)
18. a (p. 277)
19. c (p. 278)
20. c (p. 279)

CHAPTER TWELVE

UNDERSTANDING ACCOUNTING AND INFORMATION SYSTEMS

CHAPTER OVERVIEW

Accounting is a comprehensive information system for collecting, analyzing, and communicating financial information. At the head of the accounting system is the controller, who manages all of the firm's accounting activities. Rules and procedures governing the content and form of financial reports follow generally accepted accounting principles (GAAP). Assets equal liabilities plus owners' equity. Accountants use a double-entry accounting system to record the dual effects of financial transactions. Two broad categories of financial statements are balance sheets and income statements. A budget is a detailed statement of estimated receipts and expenditures for a period of time in the future. Ratios to be used in financial statement analysis are normally grouped into three major classifications: solvency, profitability, and activity ratios. Information management is an internal operation that determines business performance and outcomes and it deals in data and information. Management information systems (MIS) are systems for transforming data into information that can be used in decision making. Most application programs used by businesses fall into one or more of these categories: word processing, spreadsheets, database management, or graphics. Artificial intelligence (AI) is the programming of computers to imitate human thought processes.

LEARNING OBJECTIVES

1. Explain the role of accountants and distinguish between the kinds of work done by public and private accountants.

2. Explain how the following concepts are used in record keeping: accounting equations, double-entry accounting, and T-accounts for debits and credits.

3. Describe the two basic financial statements and show how they reflect the activity and financial condition of a business.

4. Explain how computing key financial ratios can help in analyzing the financial strengths of a business.

5. Identify the role played in computer systems by databases and application programs.

6. Classify computer systems by size and structure.

7. List some trends in the application of computer technology for business information management.

DISCUSSION OF OPENING VIGNETTE

In its splendid exposition of how computers are becoming more and more capable of providing pertinent information instantly, the opening vignette brings up an important issue: right of privacy. Like any other issue, this one has two sides. First, let's consider it from the viewpoint of someone who wants to guard that right to privacy. In the future you may apply for a job with a prestigious firm. Your second interview is going quite well when your potential supervisor says: "Pardon me just a moment, I want to punch up your college record." Within seconds, that potential supervisor has on his or her screen your transcript of grades, your disciplinary record, and some rather personal data from your college years. You are mad and say: "You have no right to that information!" For people who have had military service, most job applications ask merely if you were honorably discharged. However, suppose you're a veteran and during a job interview the interviewer calls up on a computer your complete set of files at the Pentagon. An item or two may be embarrassing to you and may threaten your chances of getting the job. Again you shout: "You have no right to that information!" Then, when you go to rent a car, you notice the clerk behind the counter is hesitating. That clerk has received via computer technology some unfavorable information about you, and you feel that the clerk does not have a right to delve into your private matters. Again, you are right! Your relations with a university, the military, or law enforcement officials should not be bandied about among the general public. But, there is a huge "however" to be inserted here. The car-rental clerk might respond: "As a person who has never met you before, I have no right to delve into your files this way. I apologize. However, when you ask to take one of our valuable cars out on the highway, it is understood that you are allowing me, then, to find out something about you." Similarly, when you apply for a job, you are saying to the potential employer, "I give you permission to find out all you can about my academic record at college." So, perhaps car rental firms have their rights, too.

1. Evaluate this statement: "Someday soon we can access a national data bank that will instantly provide complete information on everyone."

2. Eloquently defend a car-rental firm's right to search your driving records.

3. What do you think of Mr. Armstrong's statement that there is no legal right to rent a car in this country.

4. What, to date, has prevented other industries from having the kind of instant information that car-rental firms are so rapidly acquiring?

ANNOTATED KEY TERMS

Accounting - Comprehensive information system for collecting, analyzing, and communicating financial information.

Accounting system - Organized means by which financial information is identified, measured, recorded, and retained for use in accounting statements and management reports.

Controller - Person who manages all of a firm's accounting activities; chief accounting officer.

Certified public accountant - Accountant licensed by the state and offering services to the public.

Audit - Systematic examination of a company's accounting system to determine whether its reports fairly present its operations.

Generally accepted accounting principles (GAAP) - Accepted rules and procedures governing the content and form of financial reports.

Management advisory services - Specialized accounting services to help managers resolve a variety of business problems.

Private accountant - Salaried accountant hired by a business to carry out its day-to-day financial services.

Certified management accountant (CMA) - Certified accountant recognized as a specialist in management accounting.

Journal - Chronological record of a firm's financial transactions, including a brief description of each.

Ledger - Record, divided into accounts and usually compiled on a monthly basis, containing summaries of all journal transactions.

Fiscal year - Twelve-month period designated for annual financial-reporting purposes.

Asset - Any economic resource expected to benefit a firm or an individual who owns it.

Liability - Debt owed by a firm to an outside organization or individual.

Owners' equity - Amount of money that owners would receive if they sold all of a firm's assets and paid all of its liabilities.

Double-entry accounting system - Bookkeeping system that balances the accounting equation by recording the dual effects of every financial transaction.

T-account - Bookkeeping format for recording transactions that takes the shape of a T whose vertical line divides the account into debits (left side) and credits (right side).

Debit - Bookkeeping entry in a T-account that records increases in assets.

Credit - Bookkeeping entry in a T-account that records decreases in assets.

Financial statement - Any of several types of records summarizing a company's financial status to aid in managerial decision making.

Balance sheet - Financial statement detailing a firm's assets, liabilities, and owners' equity.

Current asset - Asset that can or will be converted into cash within the following year.

Liquidity - Ease with which an asset can be converted into cash.

Accounts receivable - Amounts due from customers who have purchased goods on credit.

Merchandise inventory - Cost of merchandise which has been acquired for sale to customers and which is still on hand.

Prepaid expense - Expense, such as prepaid rent, that is paid before the upcoming period in which it is due.

Fixed asset - Asset with long-term use or value, such as land, buildings, and equipment.

Depreciation - Process of distributing the cost of an asset over its life.

Intangible asset - Nonphysical asset, such as a patent or trademark, that has economic value in the form of expected benefit.

Goodwill - Amount paid for an existing business above the value of its own assets.

Current liability - Debt that must be paid within one year.

Accounts payable - Unpaid bills owed to suppliers, plus wages and taxes due within the upcoming year.

Long-term liability - Debt that is not due for more than one year.

Paid-in capital - Additional money, above proceeds from stock sale, paid directly to a firm by its owners.

Retained earnings - Earnings retained by a firm for its use rather than paid as dividends.

Income statement (or profit-and-loss statement) - Financial statement listing a firm's annual revenues and expenses so that a "bottom line" shows annual profit or loss.

Revenues - Funds that flow into a business from the sale of goods and services.

Cost of goods sold - Total cost of obtaining materials for making the products sold by a firm during the year.

Gross profit (gross margin) - Revenues from goods sold minus cost of goods sold.

Operating expenses - Costs, other than the cost of goods sold, incurred in producing a good or service.

Operating income - Gross profit minus operating expenses.

Net income (or net profit or net earnings) - Gross profit minus operating expenses and income taxes.

Statement of cash flows - Financial statement describing a firm's yearly cash receipts and cash payments.

Budget - Detailed statement of estimated receipts and expenditures for a period of time in the future.

Solvency ratio - Financial ratio, both short- and long-term, for estimating the risk in investing in a firm.

Profitability ratio - Financial ratio for measuring a firm's potential earnings.

Activity ratio - Financial ratio for evaluating management's use of a firm's assets.

Liquidity ratio - Solvency ratio measuring a firm's ability to pay its immediate debts.

Current ratio - Solvency ratio that determines a firm's creditworthiness by measuring its ability to pay current liabilities.

Working capital - Difference between a firm's current assets and current liabilities.

Debt ratio - Solvency ratio measuring a firm's ability to meet its long-term debts.

Debt-to-owners' equity ratio (or debt-to-equity ratio) - Solvency ratio describing the extent to which a firm is financed through borrowing.

Debt - A firm's total liabilities.

Leverage - Ability to finance an investment through borrowed funds.

Return on investment (or return on equity) - Profitability ratio measuring income earned for each dollar invested.

Earnings per share - Profitability ratio measuring the size of the dividend that a firm can pay shareholders.

Activity ratio - Financial ratio measuring how efficiently a firm uses its resources in generating profit.

Inventory turnover ratio - Activity ratio measuring the average number of times that inventory is sold and restocked during the year.

Data - Raw facts and figures.

Information - The meaningful, useful interpretation of data.

Management information system - System for transforming raw data into information that can be used in decision making.

Hardware - Physical components of a computer system.

Software - Programs that instruct a computer in what to do.

Program - Set of instructions used by a computer to perform specified activities.

Database - Centralized, organized collection of related data.

Batch processing - Method of collecting data over a period of time and then computer-processing them as a group or batch.

Real-time processing - Method of entering data and computer processing them immediately.

Word-processing program - Application program that allows computers to store, edit, and print letters and numbers for documents created by users.

Database management program - Application program for creating, storing, searching, and manipulating an organized collection of data.

Microcomputer (or personal computer) - Smallest, slowest, least expensive form of computer.

Minicomputer - Computer whose capacity, speed, and cost fall between those of microcomputers and mainframes.

Mainframe - Computer whose capacity and speed enable it to service many users simultaneously.

Supercomputer - Largest, fastest, most expensive form of computer.

Systems architecture - Location of a computer system's elements-- data-entry and data-processing operations, database, data output, and computer staff.

Centralized system - Form of computer-system architecture in which all processing is done in one location through a centralized computer, database, and staff.

Decentralized system - Form of computer-system architecture in which processing is done in many locations by means of separate computers, databases, and personnel.

Computer network - Group of interconnected computer systems able to exchange information with one another from different locations.

Wide area network - Network of computers and work stations linked by telephone wires or by satellite.

Local area network (LAN) - Network of computers and workstations, usually within a company, linked together by cable.

Artificial intelligence (AI) - Construction and programming of computers to imitate human thought processes.

Expert system - Form of artificial intelligence that attempts to imitate the behavior of human experts in a particular field.

Fax machine - Machine that can transmit copies of documents (text and graphics) over telephone lines.

Electronic mail (E-mail) - Computer system that electronically transmits letters, reports, and other information between computers.

TRUE-FALSE QUESTIONS

1. Accounting is a comprehensive information system for collecting, analyzing, and communicating financial information.

2. Private accountants are almost always independent of the firms they audit.

3. When an asset increases, it is entered as a credit.

4. It would make sense that assets minus liabilities would equal owners' equity.

5. Income statements supply detailed information on the accounting-equation factors: assets, liabilities, and owners' equity.

6. Accounts receivable are amounts due from customers who have purchased goods on credit.

7. Goodwill is the amount paid for an existing business over and above the value of its assets.

8. Goodwill results from public relations expenditures and thus will be found only on the income statement of a firm.

9. Common stocks, paid-in capital, and retained earnings are categories that may be found listed under owners' equity.

10. In accounting terminology, revenues and net income mean the same thing.

MULTIPLE CHOICE QUESTIONS

1. Who, according to the textbook, is at the head of the accounting system of a firm?

    a. vice president for finance
    b. controller
    c. bookkeeper
    d. CEO

2. Who or what governs the content and form of financial reports?

    a. controller
    b. Federal government
    c. state statutes
    d. GAAP

3. Which of the following is NOT usually considered to be part of the accounting equation?

   a. expenses
   b. owners' equity
   c. assets
   d. liabilities

4. One of the following choices below is an alternative way of referring to the balance sheet. Which item is it?

   a. statement of cash flows
   b. profit-and-loss statement
   c. statement of financial position
   d. cash equivalency statement

5. Which one of the following will NOT be a part of a balance sheet?

   a. accounts receivable
   b. cost of goods sold
   c. owners' equity
   d. intangible assets

6. Which one of the following will NOT be a part of an income statement?

   a. cost of goods sold
   b. goodwill
   c. revenues
   d. operating expenses

7. The textbook has treated several kinds of ratios. Listed below are three of those classifications along with an impostor. Indicate the inappropriate item.

   a. socio-economic ratios
   b. solvency ratios
   c. profitability ratios
   d. activity ratios

8. It is defined as the difference between the firm's current assets and its current liabilities. What is it?

   a. the profitability quotient
   b. net income
   c. degree of flexibility
   d. working capital

9. How is the current ratio (often called the "bankers' ratio") calculated?

   a. net income divided by total investment
   b. current assets divided by current revenues
   c. current assets divided by current liabilities
   d. net income divided by sales

10. Select from the choices below the best short definition of the term "data" as used in the context of computers and management information systems.

   a. useful interpretation of information
   b. basic essentials for information services
   c. raw facts and figures
   d. programmatic essentials of a system

11. What do we call the process by which data are collected over some period of time and processed as groups?

   a. batch processing
   b. delayed early warning (DEW)
   c. real-time processing
   d. management of inflow

12. Each location determines the needs of its own system: physical components, programs, databases, personnel, etc. This describes which type of system?

   a. centralized
   b. decentralized
   c. network
   d. LAN

13. As you roam around the offices of a major firm, most of the computers that you will see sitting on desks are--

   a. mainframes
   b. supercomputers
   c. minicomputers
   d. microcomputers

14. The location of the various parts of the system--its data-entry and data-processing operations, database, data output, and computer staff. The term for this is--

   a. local area network
   b. logistical control design
   c. wide area network
   d. systems architecture

15. On television's Home Shopping Network, hundreds of operators seated at monitors in a large room are united via a--

    a. satellite hookup
    b. coaxial cable
    c. local area network
    d. management information system

16. Expert systems and robotics, exciting new developments in the world of computers, would both be classified under the more general heading of--

    a. artificial intelligence
    b. the computerized assembly line
    c. management information systems
    d. second generation computers

17. The textbook relates that they supply everyday users with "instant expertise." What are they?

    a. MIS bulletins
    b. expert systems
    c. real-time outputs
    d. fax machines

18. The textbook reports: "As the ratio gets larger, stock value increases. Investors know that the firm can better afford to pay dividends." Which ratio is referred to here?

    a. current ratio
    b. inventory turnover
    c. number of shares outstanding
    d. earnings per share

19. From the short list below, please select an acceptable alternate way to refer to long-term solvency ratios.

    a. profitability ratios
    b. social ratios
    c. debt ratios
    d. responsibility quotients

20. This relationship reflects a firm's ability to generate cash to meet obligations through the normal, orderly process of selling inventories and collecting accounts receivable. It is the--

    a. current ratio
    b. debt-to-equity ratio
    c. asset-liability relationship (ALR)
    d. rule of thumb

WRITING TO LEARN

1. Using strictly your own individual means of expression and creating new terminology if you wish, explain the importance of accounting to business today.

2. Consider the accounting equation. Explain, using multiple examples, the essence of each part of that famous equation.

3. "If you don't know how well you're doing, then how will you ever know if you are getting close to your goal?" Relate the preceding statement to the profession of accounting.

4. Tell of the general importance of profitability ratios. Then, go ahead to explain each of them.

5. The balance sheet and the income statement are both important documents of a firm. Tell how they differ from one another.

6. Using numerous examples, expound upon how current assets differ from fixed assets. Do you feel that we can say one group is more important to a firm than the other? Why or why not?

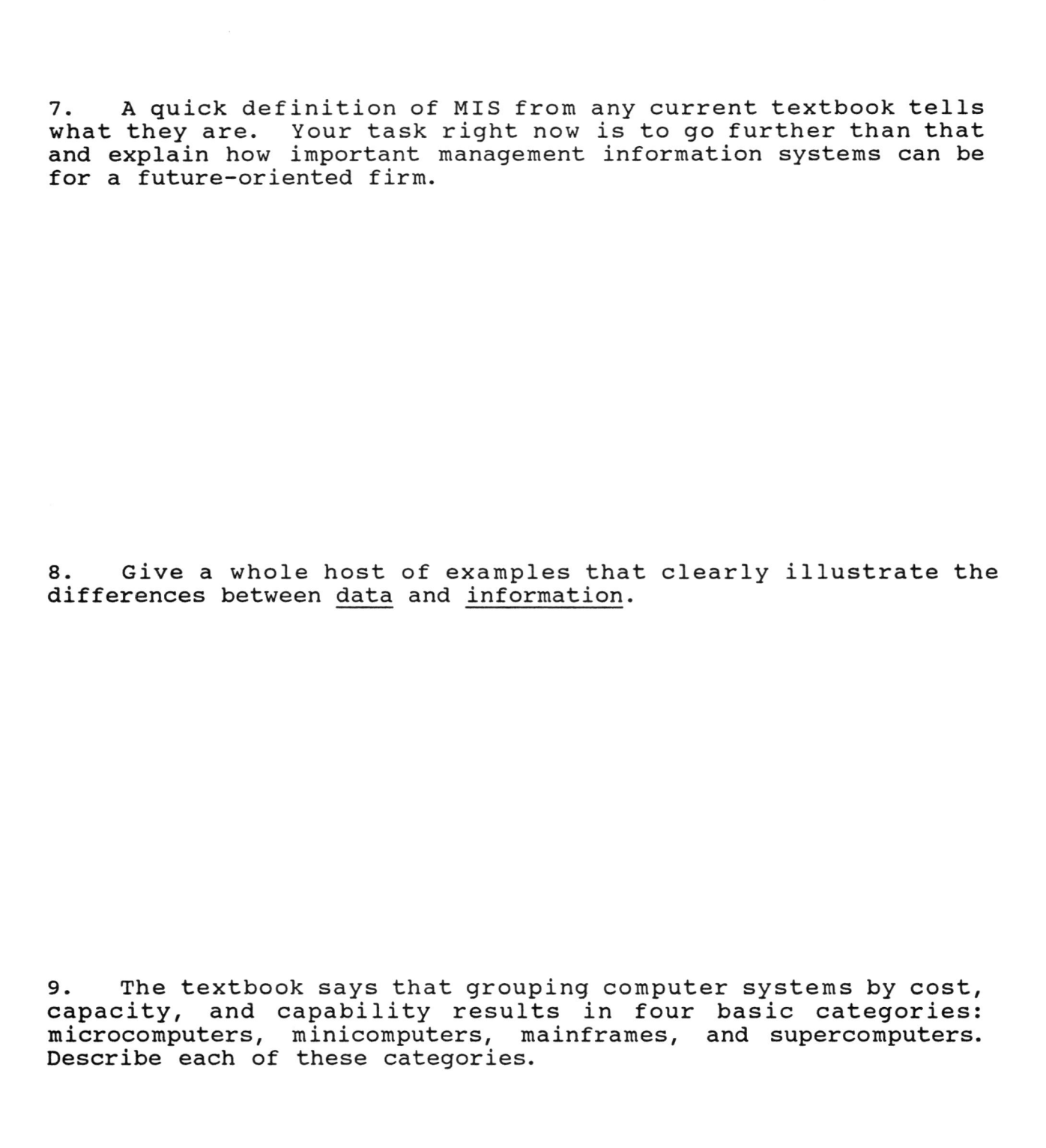

7. A quick definition of MIS from any current textbook tells what they are. Your task right now is to go further than that and explain how important management information systems can be for a future-oriented firm.

8. Give a whole host of examples that clearly illustrate the differences between _data_ and _information_.

9. The textbook says that grouping computer systems by cost, capacity, and capability results in four basic categories: microcomputers, minicomputers, mainframes, and supercomputers. Describe each of these categories.

DISCUSSION OF BUSINESS CASE 12

The Leslie Fay case makes clear that although computers and accounting procedures are inherently "honest," the human beings who make use of them might not always be quite so ethical. In the ancient days of pen-and-paper accounting, it was taught that expenditures of money should involve several people. This was a safeguard against what Professor Howard Schilit would call "shenanigans." Here is an overly-complete example of how the system worked. Melvin Mosk needed fifty dollars to cover travel expenses for a short trip he was making for the company. He first filled out a request form that was approved by Person 1. For the form to receive full blessing, it had to be approved and endorsed by Person 2. Upon receiving this twice-approved form, Person 3 would make out a payment voucher. To be valid, the voucher had to be signed by Person 4. The voucher was good only within the firm, so Melvin had to get it turned into cash. He took the voucher to Person 5, who then gave Melvin his fifty dollars. If Melvin had wanted to cheat the company, look at all the hurdles he would have to go through. It would be impossible! Often, when we computerize a firm, these "old fashioned" security measures are forgotten, and a clever hacker can pull any number of stunts. But note that in the Leslie Fay case, there were twenty people working with the controller in what has been termed "collusive fraud." So, at Leslie Fay, a Melvin Mosk could pull off a "shenanigan" if he could just get those 5 other persons to join him in the caper. Well, if you have collusive fraud, then shouldn't an audit--internal or external--pick it up? Apparently we cannot count on that happening. On many previous occasions, major accounting firms have been accused of being less than efficient in an audit. After the Leslie Fay affair, it would seem that auditing firms would want to devise methods that ensure that nothing escapes the eagle eyes of an auditing team. To use magician's terminology, we could say that at Leslie Fay the controller's hands were quicker than the auditors' eyes.

1.   The narrative says it has not been determined "why the scheme was carried out in the first place." Give your own version of why.

2.   Has this chapter led you to believe that computers can be programmed to catch what was happening at Leslie Fay? Why or why not?

3.   Do you think that an expert system can be designed to have all the human characteristics of a private investigator? How could such a system have helped in the Leslie Fay situation?

4.   Explain what you think is meant by the term "collusive fraud."

ANSWERS TO TRUE-FALSE QUESTIONS

1. T (p. 285)
2. F (p. 286)
3. F (p. 290)
4. T (p. 289)
5. F (p. 290)
6. T (p. 291)
7. T (p. 292)
8. F (p. 292)
9. T (p. 292)
10. F (p. 293)

ANSWERS TO MULTIPLE CHOICE QUESTIONS

1. b (p. 286)
2. d (p. 286)
3. a (p. 288)
4. c (p. 290)
5. b (p. 291-292)
6. b (p. 292-293)
7. a (p. 296)
8. d (p. 296)
9. c (p. 296)
10. c (p. 300)
11. a (p. 301)
12. b (p. 304)
13. d (p. 301-302)
14. d (p. 302, 304)
15. c (p. 304)
16. a (p. 305)
17. b (p. 305)
18. d (p. 297)
19. c (p. 297)
20. a (p. 296)

CHAPTER THIRTEEN

UNDERSTANDING MARKETING PROCESSES AND CONSUMER BEHAVIOR

CHAPTER OVERVIEW

Marketing is the process of planning and executing the conception, pricing, promotion, and distribution of ideas, goods, and services to create exchanges that satisfy individual and organizational objectives. Marketing can apply to consumer goods as well as industrial goods. The marketing plan is a detailed and focused strategy for gearing the marketing mix to meet consumer needs and wants. The marketing mix consists of the product, pricing, promotion, and place. Product differentiation is the creation of a product or product image that differs enough from existing products to attract customers. Within promotion, there are advertising, personal selling, sales promotions, and public relations. The marketing concept is the principle that suppliers of goods and services should focus on the wants and needs of buyers. Target markets are groups of people with similar wants and needs. Market segmentation means dividing a market into categories of customer types, or "segments." In identifying market segments, four variables are: geographic, demographic, psychographic, and product use. Market research is the study of what buyers need and how best to meet those needs. The four major influences on consumer behavior are: psychological, personal, social, and cultural.

LEARNING OBJECTIVES

1. Define marketing and explain its functions.

2. Explain market segmentation and show how it is used in target marketing.

3. Explain the purpose and value of market research.

4. Describe the key factors that influence the consumer buying process.

5. Explain how international and cultural differences affect marketing strategies.

6. Identify potential problems and opportunities in the marketing activities of small business.

DISCUSSION OF OPENING VIGNETTE

The tale of Dan and Tim Price and their Send-a-Song is a splendid vehicle for taking a first peek at market research into consumer behavior. Notice that the brothers first developed their product in its complete array of 125 songs. Then, they began researching the market. Were the first two steps taken in reverse order? That's a hard query to answer, kind of like the chicken-or-the-egg question. To conduct market research on Send-a-Song, a version of the product must be available. On the other hand, before developing a product, good marketing theory would dictate that you need consumer input first. Note that as Valentine's Day approached, Send-a-Song turned to public relations, and the new firm was fortunate enough to get a play in USA Today. Different from paid advertising in a pre-allotted space or time, public relations and publicity must depend upon the whim of editors and the relative importance they give to your publicity. Let us say that your firm was told a full one-page feature story about the firm would appear in a major newspaper on Monday, December 8, 1941. This publicity wouldn't cost your firm a penny! But when that date rolled around, allocation of news and feature space was drastically adjusted to permit coverage of the bombing of Pearl Harbor by the Japanese. Your publicity would go down the drain. Send-a-Song was lucky. At last report, acceptance of futuristic Send-a-Song service has been gratifying but spotty. Is it possible that this service is too futuristic, and consumers as a whole just don't quite know what to do with it? Also, take a moment to consider a firm whose volume of business must depend largely upon special holidays. This brings back memories of a famous classic film with Bing Crosby and Fred Astaire called "Holiday Inn," the story of a night club way out in the country that would be open only on the evenings of major holidays. From a practical standpoint, how could a night club hire a kitchen and serving staff, an orchestra, parking lot attendants, and entertainers and pay them from the revenues coming from just 20 nights per year and ever expect to make a profit?

1. Is it fair to compare Send-a-Song with the "Holiday Inn" of the motion pictures? Why or why not?

2. Develop at least one suggestion for Dan and Tim Price that could help them get Send-a-Song over the hump.

3. List at least two negative aspects that are making it difficult for Send-a-Song to get its operation into the black.

4. React to this statement: "The only problem with Send-a-Song is that it doesn't have enough songs to choose from."

ANNOTATED KEY TERMS

Marketing - The process of planning and executing the conception, pricing, promotion and distribution of goods, services, and ideas to create exchanges that satisfy individual and organizational objectives.

Consumer goods - Products purchased by consumers for personal use.

Industrial goods - Products purchased by companies to produce other products.

Marketing mix - The combination of product, pricing, promotion, and distribution strategies used to market products.

Marketing manager - Manager who plans and implements the marketing mix activities that result in the transfer of products from producer to consumer.

Marketing concept - Principle that suppliers of goods and services should focus on the wants and needs of buyers.

Marketing plan - Detailed and focused strategy for gearing the marketing mix to meet consumer needs and wants.

Product - Good, service, or idea that is marketed to fill consumer needs and wants.

Product differentiation - Creation of a product or product image that differs enough from existing products to attract consumers.

Pricing - Part of the marketing mix concerned with selecting the appropriate prices for products.

Promotion - Part of the marketing mix concerned with selecting appropriate techniques to sell products.

Advertising - Any form of paid nonpersonal communication used by an identified sponsor to persuade or inform certain audiences about a product.

Personal selling - Promotional technique that uses person-to-person communication to sell products.

Sales promotion - Promotional technique involving one-time direct inducements (such as coupons, trading stamps, and package inserts) to market a product.

Public relations - All promotional activities directed at building good relations with various sectors of the population.

Publicity - Communication to the public (usually through the mass media) about a product or firm over which the firm has no control.

<u>Distribution</u> - Part of the marketing mix concerned with getting products from producers to consumers.

<u>Exchange</u> - Any transaction in which two or more parties trade things of value.

<u>Target market</u> - Group of people who have similar wants and needs and who can be expected to show interest in the same products.

<u>Market segmentation</u> - Process of dividing a market into categories of customer types.

<u>Positioning</u> - Process of fixing, adapting, and communicating the nature of a product.

<u>Geographic variables</u> - Geographical units that may be considered in developing a segmentation strategy.

<u>Demographic variables</u> - Characteristics of populations that may be considered in developing a segmentation.

<u>Product-use variables</u> - Consumer characteristics based on the ways in which a product is used, the brand loyalty it enjoys, and the reasons for which it is purchased.

<u>Psychographic variables</u> - Consumer characteristics, such as lifestyles, opinions, interests, and attitudes, that may be considered in developing a segmentation strategy.

<u>Market research</u> - The study of consumer needs and wants and the ways in which sellers can best meet them.

<u>Secondary data</u> - Data readily available as a result of previous research.

<u>Primary data</u> - Data developed through new research.

<u>Observation</u> - Market research technique that involves simply watching and recording consumer behavior.

<u>Survey</u> - Market research technique using a questionnaire that is either mailed to individuals or used as the basis of interviews.

<u>Focus group</u> - Market research technique in which a group of individuals is gathered, presented with an issue, and asked to discuss it in depth.

<u>Experimentation</u> - Market research technique that attempts to compare the responses of the same or similar individuals under different circumstances.

<u>Consumer behavior</u> - The various facets of the decision process by which customers come to purchase and consume products.

__Rational motives__ - Reasons for purchasing a product that are based on a logical evaluation of product attributes.

__Emotional motives__ - Reasons for purchasing a product that are based on nonobjective factors.

TRUE-FALSE QUESTIONS

1. Marketing is the process of planning and executing the conception, pricing, promotion, and distribution of ideas, goods, and services to create exchanges that satisfy individual and organizational objectives.

2. Actually, industrial goods are a subcategory under consumer goods.

3. The marketing mix consists of product, pricing, promotion, and production.

4. Product differentiation is the creation of a product or product image that differs enough from existing products to attract consumers.

5. Low prices usually limit market size but they also increase profits per unit.

6. The most highly visible component of the marketing mix is no doubt promotion.

7. The marketing concept is a principle that states that you can convince any buyer to buy any product if you promote that product enough.

8. One of the four most important variables in market segmentation is that of health habits.

9. In many cases, buying decisions are affected by the places that people call home.

10. Market research is the study of what buyers need and how best to meet those needs.

MULTIPLE CHOICE QUESTIONS

1. It is defined as the process of planning and executing the conception, pricing, promotion, and distribution of ideas, goods, and services to create exchanges that satisfy individual and organizational objectives. What is it?

   a. market segmentation
   b. promotion
   c. marketing
   d. market research

2. It is defined as a detailed and focused strategy for gearing the marketing mix to meet consumer needs and wants. What is it?

    a. market segmentation
    b. marketing plan
    c. promotion
    d. advance pricing

3. Which one of the following is an element in the marketing mix?

    a. production
    b. planning
    c. pricing
    d. preparation

4. Which one of the following is NOT an element in the marketing mix?

    a. planning
    b. product
    c. promotion
    d. place

5. When a firm creates a product that can be so easily distinguished from products of other firms in an effort to attract customers, then that firm has engaged successfully in--

    a. relativistic promotion
    b. product differentiation
    c. skimming
    d. advertising

6. Which one of the following characteristics best differentiates personal selling from advertising?

    a. personal selling promotes the product
    b. personal selling utilizes the mass media
    c. personal selling is on a person-to-person basis
    d. personal selling can help to increase sales

7. Which one of the following is NOT a characteristic of publicity?

    a. paid for by the firm
    b. can sometimes hurt a business
    c. not controlled by the firm
    d. "free" to the firm

8. In 1985, Coca-Cola sold Coke to Eastern European and Asian countries in return for what?

   a. steel
   b. rice products
   c. fine carpets and towels
   d. bathtubs and honey

9. It is the principle that suppliers of goods and services should focus on the wants and needs of buyers. What is this principle called?

   a. market segmentation
   b. satisfaction and utility
   c. reference to consumers
   d. the marketing concept

10. When a firm divides a market into categories of customer types, we call that process--

    a. in-depth categorization
    b. market segmentation
    c. skimming
    d. market penetration

11. It is any transaction in which two or more parties trade things of value. The textbook calls it--

    a. equalizing profit
    b. marketing bilateralism
    c. exchange
    d. consideration

12. In the list below will be found three of the four most important variables used in market segmentation, along with an inappropriate item. Please identify the item that is out of place.

    a. geographic
    b. demographic
    c. product use
    d. sociographic

13. According to the textbook, Procter & Gamble developed Ultra Pampers in order to better accommodate--

    a. limited storage space in Japan
    b. Southern tastes in such matters
    c. the crying of babies
    d. revised federal health standards

14. In the market research process, which one of the following steps comes earliest?

    a. prepare a report
    b. collect data
    c. analyze data
    d. select a research method

15. In market research, which one of the following steps comes **first**?

    a. study the current situation
    b. analyze the data
    c. select a research method
    d. collect the data

16. In market research, which one of the following steps comes **last**?

    a. analyze the data
    b. prepare a report
    c. select a research method
    d. study the current situation

17. Which one of the following is NOT one of the four major influences on consumer behavior, according to the textbook?

    a. psychological
    b. physical
    c. social
    d. personal

18. Which kind of influences include family, opinion leaders (people whose opinions are sought by others), and reference groups such as friends, co-workers, and professional associates?

    a. psychological
    b. personal
    c. social
    d. cultural

19. They involve nonobjective factors and can lead to "irrational" decisions. They are referred to in the textbook as--

    a. rational motives
    b. love-object motives
    c. motivating motives
    d. emotional motives

20. Although McDonald's Big Mac sells for around $2.00 in the United States, in Japan it sells for--

   a. $1.00
   b. $5.00
   c. $8.00
   d. over $10.00

WRITING TO LEARN

1. Strictly using your own vocabulary and terminology, define marketing and show what a broad area of activity it covers.

2. Explain several ways in which consumer marketing differs from industrial marketing. Begin by a simple definition of each.

3. From the marketing mix, select the concept of "place" and then go on to persuade your reader that it is indeed the most important member of the marketing mix.

4. Respond to this comment: "There is really no such thing as product differentiation. All products of a given sort are alike, and any 'differences' are strictly in the mind of the consumer."

5. Using numerous illustrations, show the differences between personal selling and sales promotion. Which do you think is more important?

6. Show how the marketing concept, if really believed by a firm, could affect everything that the firm does.

7. Write a set of Five Commandments to be observed by an honest advertiser. For at least two of the Five Commandments, give examples of how they have been violated in the past.

8. The textbook says: "Target marketing clearly requires market segmentation." Develop a narrative that explains what this statement means.

9. Convince your reader of the supreme importance of taking into consideration demographic variables. Utilize a multitude of illustrations.

DISCUSSION OF BUSINESS CASE 13

The narrative concerning supermarket shelves provides a splendid example of a particular facet of market research in action. More importantly, the piece displays some of the dangers in trying to get inside the heads of consumers. First, the narrative admits that some patrons find in-store audio commercials to be "intrusive and annoying." It's possible that some customers may decide to buy from a market where they are NOT bombarded by such messages. Second, there is much to be said for a store that offers dependability. To enhance a sense of dependability, many supermarket chains lay out all their stores in identical fashion. This means that if the Ajax store at Chestnut and Main has dairy products in the southeast corner next to flowers, then that is the exact spot where you'll find dairy products in the store at 75th and Belmont--in the southeast corner! When you want a half gallon of milk in a hurry at Ajax, you know exactly where to run. However, when some night in a hurry you run in and find the southeast corner is now the greeting card shop, you are frustrated. "Good heavens, what have they done with the dairy products?" you ask. The answer is: "We're doing a little market research and we have concluded in our final report that the greeting card shop located there in the southeast corner is the most efficient use of space." As a consumer at Ajax, you are more than likely totally unimpressed by their research efforts. In fact, you resent such efforts. And that brings us to the third point. Dr. B.F. Skinner has done extensive research with rats and pigeons, manipulating their behavior with reinforcement through food pellets. Some disciples of Dr. Skinner maintain that human behavior can be manipulated or "modified" just the way Skinner did with his little pets. However, some humans can become resentful if they suspect that someone is manipulating them, especially if the manipulator is not a professional psychologist but instead just a supermarket manager. Researchers beware.

1. Objectively discuss the positive and negative aspects of in-store announcements over the public address system in between musical numbers.

2. How important do you feel "dependability" (as discussed above) is for a supermarket chain? Do people really mind hunting for merchandise that has been moved to another shelf in another part of the store? Why or why not?

3. Explain this remark from the textbook narrative: "A crazy-quilt pattern isn't consumer-friendly."

4. Within the spirit of Business Case 13, react to this remark: "If it isn't broken, then don't try to fix it!"

ANSWERS TO TRUE-FALSE QUESTIONS

1. T (p. 316)
2. F (p. 317)
3. F (p. 319)
4. T (p. 319)
5. F (p. 320)
6. T (p. 320)
7. F (p. 321)
8. F (p. 323)
9. T (p. 323)
10. T (p. 326)

ANSWERS TO MULTIPLE CHOICE QUESTIONS

1. c (p. 316)
2. b (p. 318)
3. c (p. 319)
4. a (p. 319)
5. b (p. 319)
6. c (p. 320)
7. a (p. 320)
8. d (p. 321)
9. d (p. 321)
10. b (p. 322)
11. c (p. 321)
12. d (p. 323)
13. a (p. 326)
14. d (p. 326-327)
15. a (p. 326-327)
16. b (p. 326-327)
17. b (p. 328)
18. c (p. 328)
19. d (p. 331)
20. d (p. 332)

CHAPTER FOURTEEN

DEVELOPING, PRICING, AND PROMOTING PRODUCTS

CHAPTER OVERVIEW

Product features are tangible qualities that a company "builds into" its products. Consumer products are commonly divided into three categories: convenience, shopping, and specialty products. Industrial products are divided into expense items and capital items. Stages in the product life cycle are introduction, growth, maturity, and decline. There are four categories in the growth-share matrix: question marks, stars, cash cows, and dogs. Branding is a process of using symbols to communicate qualities of a particular product made by a particular producer. Brands are developed in order to cause brand loyalty. The exclusive legal right to use a brand name is called a trademark. Patents provide legal monopolies for the use and licensing of manufactured items, processes, substances and designs. Two major objectives of pricing are profit maximizing and gaining market share. A firm has three options for pricing existing products-- above market, below market, or at market. For new products, there are price skimming and penetration pricing. Some pricing tactics are price lining, psychological pricing, and discounting. The promotional mix contains four types of promotional tools: advertising, personal selling, sales promotions, and publicity-public relations.

LEARNING OBJECTIVES

1. Identify a product and distinguish between consumer and industrial products.

2. Trace the stages of the product life cycle and explain the growth-share matrix.

3. Discuss the importance of branding and packaging.

4. Identify the various pricing objectives that govern pricing decisions and describe the tools used in making these decisions.

5. Discuss pricing strategies and tactics for existing and new products.

6. Identify the objectives of promotion and discuss the considerations involved in selecting a promotional mix.

7. Describe the various advertising media available to marketing managers.

8. Identify the different types of sales promotions and explain the uses of publicity and public relations.

DISCUSSION OF OPENING VIGNETTE

As we peruse the narrative on Procter & Gamble, we must constantly remind ourselves that what P&G Chairman Edwin Artzt did for Procter and Gamble was appropriate for P&G, but might NOT be appropriate for other companies. Artzt knew his company and knew the environment in which it functioned and picked what he felt were the right tactics and strategies. To sum things up quickly, he put great emphasis on offering P&G products at the lowest possible prices. There is a mention that these are "cost-conscious times" for consumers. Well, for some consumers the times will always be cost-conscious. The key to the hearts of such customers is maintaining the lowest price in the market. Notice that in concert with lowering P&G prices, Artzt reduced the flow of coupons and cut back on allowances to retailers. With some consumers this first P&G action would be a fatal mistake. Many intelligent consumers religiously clip coupons, keep large filing systems filled with them, make careful note of expiration dates, and often let special coupon offers guide their shopping on trips to the supermarket. In today's terminology, we could say that for those particular consumers, purchases are "coupon-driven." Before any firm reduces its coupon effort, it should carefully assess the impact of the coupon trade on their sales. Then, there's the trimming of discounts to retail stores. A firm such as P&G does not want to do anything that would tend to alienate the retailers. A firm should never tighten up on the retailers without knowing in advance what the impact will be. Also, there's the matter of making a little tin god out of low prices. With some products, a higher price makes a product more attractive. That's not a typographical error; it's true. Take perfume, for example. If a major fragrance manufacturer offered a quart of "Nights under Indonesian Palms" for five dollars, it probably would not sell very well. But put a fraction of a pint of "Nights under Indonesian Palms" in a fancy bottle and it will sell well for perhaps forty-five dollars a bottle. Chances are, though, Mr. Artzt knows what he is doing.

1. Is Mr. Artzt acting wisely in making light of the sales impact of coupons? Why or why not?

2. If you were a retailer and P&G cut allowances to you, would you be tempted to reduce the shelf space allotted to Procter & Gamble? Explain.

3. If Procter & Gamble became known as the "low-price leader," do you feel P&G could cut back on its advertising? NOTE: In most years, P&G is the major advertiser in the U.S.

4. Using percents in your response, tell how many consumers shop for the lowest price as opposed to those consumers who shop for quality.

ANNOTATED KEY TERMS

Feature - Tangible quality that a company "builds into" a product.

Convenience good/service - Relatively inexpensive product purchased and consumed rapidly and regularly.

Shopping good/service - Moderately expensive, infrequently purchased product.

Specialty good/service - Expensive, rarely purchased product.

Expense item - Relatively inexpensive industrial product purchased and consumed rapidly and regularly.

Capital item - Expensive, durable, infrequently purchased industrial product such as a building.

Product mix - Group of products that a firm makes available for sale.

Product line - Group of similar products intended for a similar group of buyers who will use them in similar ways.

Speed to market - Strategy of introducing new products to respond quickly to customer and/or market changes.

Product life cycle (PLC) - Series of stages in a product's profit-producing life.

Growth-share matrix - System for classifying products according to market share and growth potential.

Branding - Process of using symbols to communicate the qualities of a product made by a particular producer.

Trademark - Exclusive legal right to use a brand name.

Patent - Exclusive right to use and license a manufactured item or substance, a manufacturing process, or an object design.

Packaging - Physical container in which a product is sold, advertised, and/or protected.

Pricing - Process of determining what a company will receive in exchange for its products.

Markup - Amount added to an item's cost to sell it at a profit.

Variable cost - Cost that changes with the quantity of a product produced or sold.

Fixed cost - Cost unaffected by the quantity of a product produced or sold.

Break-even analysis - Assessment of the quantity of a product that must be sold before the seller makes a profit.

Break-even point - Quantity of a product that must be sold before the seller covers variable and fixed costs and makes a profit.

Price leader - Dominant firm that establishes product prices that other companies follow.

Price skimming - Setting an initial high price to cover new-product costs and to generate a profit.

Penetration pricing - Setting an initial low price to establish a new product in the market.

Price lining - Setting a limited number of prices for certain categories of products.

Psychological pricing - Pricing tactic that takes advantage of consumers not always responding rationally to stated prices.

Odd-even pricing - Psychological pricing tactic based on the premise that customers prefer prices not stated in even dollar amounts.

Discount - Price reduction offered as an incentive to purchase.

Promotion - Aspect of the marketing mix concerned with the most effective techniques for selling a product.

Positioning - Process of establishing an identifiable product image in the minds of consumers.

Pull strategy - Promotional strategy designed to appeal directly to customers who will demand a product.

Push strategy - Promotional strategy designed to appeal directly to customers who will demand a product from retailers.

Promotional mix - Combination of tools used to promote a product.

Advertising - Promotional tool consisting of paid, nonpersonal communication from an identified sponsor to inform an audience about a product.

Advertising media - Variety of communication devices for carrying a seller's message to potential customers.

Media mix - Combination of advertising media chosen to carry messages about a product.

Direct mail - Advertising medium in which messages are mailed directly to consumers' homes or places of business.

Personal selling - Promotional tool in which a salesperson communicates one-on-one with potential customers.

Telemarketing - Form of personal selling in which telephone solicitors are used to contact customers.

Sales promotion - Short-term promotional activity designed to stimulate consumer buying or cooperation from distributors and sales agents.

Coupon - Sales promotion technique in which a certificate that entitles the buyer to a reduced price is issued.

Point-of-purchase (POP) display - Sales promotion technique in which product displays are located in certain areas to stimulate purchase.

Premium - Sales promotion technique in which offers of free or reduced-price items are used to stimulate purchase.

Trade show - Sales promotion technique in which various members of an industry gather to display, demonstrate, and sell products.

Publicity - Promotional tool in which information about a company or product is transmitted by general mass media.

Public relations - Company-influenced publicity directed at building goodwill between an organization and potential customers.

TRUE-FALSE QUESTIONS

1. Product features are tangible qualities that a company "builds into" its products.

2. Shopping goods are consumed rapidly and regularly.

3. Newspapers and a fast-food hamburger are considered to be specialty goods.

4. In the world of industrial products and services, the term "expense item" refers to expensive, long-lasting goods and services.

5. A firm's success at responding to customer demand or market changes is referred to as speed to market.

6. As might be suspected, the "growth" stage in the product life cycle begins when the product reaches the marketplace.

7. A product is referred to as a "cash cow" if it has high market share and high growth potential.

8. A producer can apply to the U.S. government for a patent-- the exclusive legal right to use a brand name.

9. Cost-oriented pricing takes into account the need to cover production costs.

10. Variable costs are costs that change with the number of goods or services produced or sold.

MULTIPLE CHOICE QUESTIONS

1. A wedding gown is an example of them as is the catering for a wedding reception--extremely important and expensive items. What are they?

    a. convenience goods and services
    b. shopping goods and services
    c. specialty goods and services
    d. industrial goods and services

2. As you and your family select a stereo system appropriate for your particular situation, you are seeking a--

    a. convenience good
    b. shopping good
    c. specialty good
    d. industrial good

3. Among industrial products, which of the following can be classified as a capital item?

    a. oil
    b. bulkloads of tea
    c. paint
    d. baking ovens

4. Among industrial products, which of the following can be classified as an expense item?

    a. buildings
    b. gloves
    c. water towers
    d. computers

5. It is referred to as a group of similar products intended for a similar group of buyers who will use them in similar ways. What is it?

    a. product line
    b. product mix
    c. product market
    d. product area

6. The Maroon Corporation manufactures small trucks, picture frames, breakfast foods, electric fixtures, sporting goods, and textbooks. This array of products is referred to as Maroon Corporation's--

    a. product line
    b. product mix
    c. product market
    d. product area

7. Orange Corporation manufactures dishwasher detergents, laundry detergents, facial soap, bath soap, and soap dispensers. This array of products is referred to as Orange Corporation's--

    a. product line
    b. product mix
    c. product market
    d. product area

8. From the list below, select the term that captures the essence of a firm's success in responding to customer demand or market changes.

    a. adaptability
    b. turnaround time
    c. speed to market
    d. customer orientation

9. Which of the stages in the product life cycle is defined as containing a slowing in sales growth. Increased competition eventually leads to price cutting and lower profits in this stage.

   a. introduction
   b. growth
   c. maturity
   d. decline

10. They have low market share, low growth potential. Profits and sales signal that the life cycle is nearly complete. Here we have described the--

    a. question marks
    b. stars
    c. cash cows
    d. dogs

11. Which of the following has high market share and high growth potential?

    a. question marks
    b. stars
    c. cash cows
    d. dogs

12. It can be said of them that they have large shares of still-growing markets. Which are they?

    a. question marks
    b. stars
    c. cash cows
    d. dogs

13. They are symbols for characterizing products and distinguishing them from one another. What are they?

    a. brand names
    b. official company colors
    c. copyrights
    d. bar codes

14. Rinso, Fab, Vitalis, and Maypo have something in common. They are all--

    a. from Procter & Gamble
    b. dogs in the growth-share matrix
    c. advertised strictly on radio
    d. manufactured in Minneapolis

15. A producer can apply to the U.S. government for the exclusive legal right to use a brand name. This legal right is referred to as--

 a. copyright
 b. patent
 c. trademark
 d. brandizing

16. A producer can obtain a legal monopoly for the use and licensing of manufactured items, manufacturing processes, substances, and designs for objects. This legal monopoly is called--

 a. brandizing
 b. exclusive distributorship
 c. trademark
 d. patent

17. It can serve as an in-store advertisement that makes the product attractive, displays the brand name, and identifies features and benefits. It reduces the risk of damage, breakage, or spoilage and increases the difficulty of stealing smaller products. What is it?

 a. package
 b. point-of-purchase display
 c. display cabinet
 d. shelf space

18. A store determines three or four price points at which a particular product will be sold. For men's suits, the price points might be $175, $250, and $400. This practice is a part of--

 a. pointing up
 b. discounting
 c. price lining
 d. price discrimination

19. The ultimate objective of any promotion is to--

 a. communicate effectively with the consumers
 b. develop strategies that will be well received
 c. increase sales
 d. increase attractiveness of packaging

20. The process of establishing an easily identifiable product image in the minds of consumers is best defined as--

 a. promotion
 b. positioning
 c. packaging
 d. market segmentation

WRITING TO LEARN

1. Define "positioning" and explain why it is so important to a firm trying to effectively market a product.

2. Using numerous examples and illustrations, explain each of the four stages of the product life cycle (PLC).

3. From the product life cycle (PLC), select your favorite stage. Then give a comprehensive treatment to what happens in that stage. Use as many illustrative examples as you can.

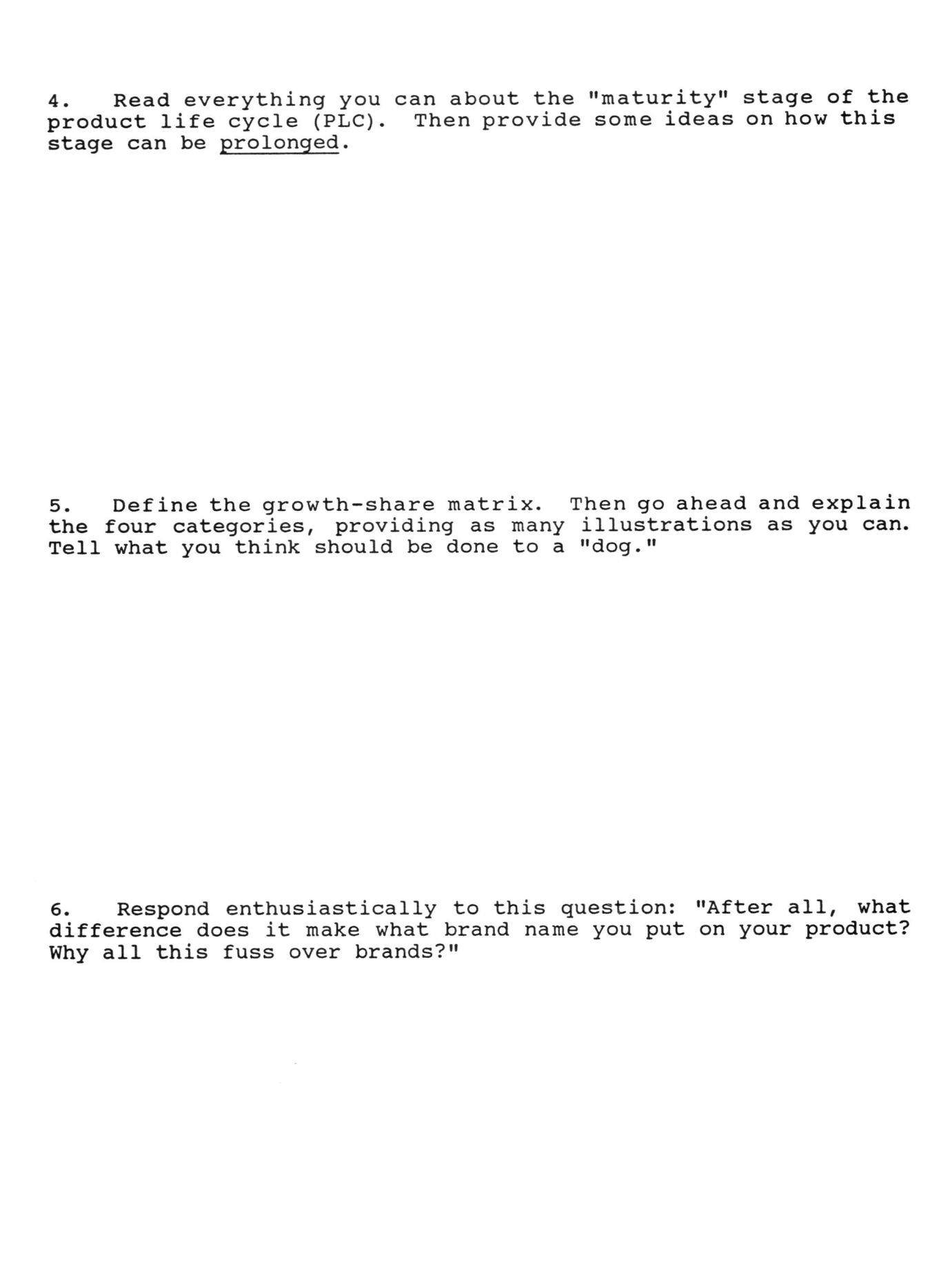

4. Read everything you can about the "maturity" stage of the product life cycle (PLC). Then provide some ideas on how this stage can be prolonged.

5. Define the growth-share matrix. Then go ahead and explain the four categories, providing as many illustrations as you can. Tell what you think should be done to a "dog."

6. Respond enthusiastically to this question: "After all, what difference does it make what brand name you put on your product? Why all this fuss over brands?"

7. Explain the difference between variable costs and fixed costs and then give examples of each. When you establish a year's advertising budget, are you dealing with fixed or variable costs?

8. What is the difference between the terms "promotion" and "advertising"? How does advertising differ from publicity? Can a product be marketed effectively without advertising? Why or why not?

9. Provide the official definitions of pull strategy and push strategy and make clear the contexts in which they are used. In doing so, provide numerous illustrations.

DISCUSSION OF BUSINESS CASE 14

The textbook discusses several approaches to pricing. Call them strategies, call them tactics, call them what you will. Implicit in what the textbook says is this warning: "Your pricing must not violate existing statutes of the venue in which you operate." Pricing can be creative and often tricky. Some clever entrepreneurs will try just about anything in the way of pricing in order to increase sales. But there is a frontier that separates "creative pricing" from illegal activity. In the State of Arkansas, the case tells us, selling an item at below the wholesale cost at which the product was acquired is illegal so long as the practice is designed to injure competitors. No doubt about it, Wal-Mart sold below cost. The narrative indicates that, for now, Wal-Mart has been ordered by a court to cease and desist such a practice. In terms of marketing, however, this case reaches far beyond just pricing practices. Ever since our days of reading Bible stories, we have identified with David at the expense of Goliath. Clearly, in this case narrative, Wal-Mart is portrayed (whether rightly or wrongly) as Goliath; that's not the kind of publicity any firm wants to receive. It's the kind of publicity that many dollars' worth of advertising will not wipe out. All of this points out that publicity can be negative as well as positive. The case narrative implies that in the Wal-Mart defense there was mention that certain items will be sold at very, very low prices, but that such items will be balanced by items not selling quite so low. As students in a business course, you should know that so-called "discount houses" can price certain items _higher_ than more mainstream retailers will price the same products. The secret to saving money at a discount house is to buy only those items with ridiculously low prices. Whether such advice applies to shopping at Wal-Mart, each shopper will have to determine individually.

1. Does this pricing case in the courts have the potential for damaging somewhat the friendly image of Wal-Mart? Why or why not?

2. Go back over the pricing strategies displayed in the textbook, and determine which of those is most appropriate for this Wal-Mart case.

3. You are in charge of promotion at Wal-Mart. Answer this accusation, whether it be fair or unfair: "You are driving the little retailer out of business."

4. If all drugstores in a small town where Wal-Mart operates go out of business, do you think Wal-Mart will continue to sell pharmacy-type items below cost? Why or why not?

ANSWERS TO TRUE-FALSE QUESTIONS

1. T (p. 343)
2. F (p. 343)
3. F (p. 343)
4. F (p. 343)
5. T (p. 346)

6. F (p. 346)
7. T (p. 347)
8. F (p. 350)
9. T (p. 352)
10. T (p. 352)

ANSWERS TO MULTIPLE CHOICE QUESTIONS

1. c (p. 343)
2. b (p. 343)
3. d (p. 344)
4. b (p. 344)
5. a (p. 344)
6. b (p. 344)
7. a (p. 344)
8. c (p. 346)
9. c (p. 346)
10. d (p. 347)

11. b (p. 347)
12. b (p. 347)
13. a (p. 348)
14. b (p. 348)
15. c (p. 350)
16. d (p. 350)
17. a (p. 350)
18. c (p. 355)
19. c (p. 356)
20. b (p. 356)

CHAPTER FIFTEEN

DISTRIBUTING GOODS AND SERVICES

CHAPTER OVERVIEW

The distribution mix is the combination of distribution channels that a firm selects to get a product to end users. Once called middlemen, intermediaries are the individuals and firms who help distribute a producer's goods. A distribution channel is the path that a product follows from producer to end user. Some strategies for distributing through channels are: intensive, exclusive, and selective distributions. Channel conflict occurs when members of the channel disagree over the roles they should play or the rewards they should receive. The channel captain is the one channel member who is most powerful in determining the roles and rewards of other members. Wholesalers are divided into two broad categories: merchant wholesalers and agents/brokers. There are full-service merchant wholesalers (including rack jobbers) and limited-function merchant wholesalers (including drop shippers). Two classifications of retail stores are product-line retailers (including department stores, supermarkets, hypermarkets, and specialty stores) and bargain retailers (including discount houses, off-price stores, catalog showrooms, and factory outlets). Major types of nonstore selling are mail marketing, video marketing, telemarketing, and electronic shopping. Possibly the oldest form of retailing, direct selling is still used by more than 600 companies.

LEARNING OBJECTIVES

1. Identify the different channels of distribution and explain different distribution strategies.

2. Explain the differences between merchant wholesalers and agents/brokers.

3. Identify the different types of retail stores.

4. Describe the major activities in the physical distribution process.

5. Compare the five basic forms of transportation and identify the types of firms that provide them.

DISCUSSION OF OPENING VIGNETTE

The underlying message that seems to rest behind each item of data revealed in this case narrative about The Gap is that changes in the market are happening continuously and constant adapting will always be necessary. To supplement the phrase "baby boomers were moving into middle age," we can allow ourselves the freedom to guess that shopping habits of college students change as those students become part of the permanent workforce. The Gap had some very successful stores in towns where major universities are located. Wearing The Gap merchandise was a part--the case suggests--of belonging to the "in" crowd. As those students graduated and moved into new peer groups, clothing from The Gap lost its significance--for them. Now, it was important for these graduates to obtain as many nice items of clothing as limited dollars could buy. The Gap just could not draw these former students back. This same phenomenon may explain why "swing music" died away. There was a time when large crowds of college-age people would turn out to hear Glenn Miller, Tommy Dorsey, Les Brown, Harry James, etc. These loyal fans continued to exist; so why didn't they keep showing up for dances? Their lifestyles had changed. Free nights were spent not going to a dance but putting the kids to bed, going to piano recitals of their children, watching Little League games, etc. Swing was still here in the world and so were the fans. But those fans had, if you will, outgrown going to a Tommy Dorsey dance. Are the dance halls and auditoriums empty and filled with spider webs today? Of course not. They are jammed with a new generation that wants, not swing, but rock music! There is perhaps no historical record of the name of the first person who said: "You know, swing bands don't bring people in anymore like they used to. We in the music business are going to have to adjust." Someone may have made a similar statement at The Gap some years ago, but the narrative suggests that no one in charge was listening.

1. Be specific and tell some of the very first signs that a store of The Gap might have noticed as indications that their clientele was slipping away.

2. How does trying to put a boost in sales at The Gap relate to the chapter's topic of distribution?

3. Above we said that as young people graduated from college they left The Gap behind. Well, what happened to the new crop of incoming college students?

4. React to this statement in relation to the challenge facing The Gap: "If you wait until everyone is certain what the trend is, then it's almost too late to make adjustments."

ANNOTATED KEY TERMS

<u>Distribution</u> <u>mix</u> - The combination of distribution channels by which a firm gets its products to end users.

<u>Intermediary</u> - Individual or firm that helps to distribute a product.

<u>Wholesaler</u> - Intermediary who sells products to other businesses for resale to final consumers.

<u>Retailer</u> - Intermediary who sells products directly to consumers.

<u>Distribution</u> <u>channel</u> - Network of interdependent companies through which a product passes from producer to end user.

<u>Direct</u> <u>channel</u> - Distribution channel in which a product travels from producer to consumer without intermediaries.

<u>Sales</u> <u>agent/broker</u> - Independent intermediary who usually represents many manufacturers and sells to wholesalers.

<u>Industrial</u> <u>distribution</u> - Network of channel members involved in the flow of manufactured goods to industrial customers.

<u>Sales</u> <u>office</u> - Office maintained by a manufacturer as a contact point with its customers.

<u>Intensive</u> <u>distribution</u> - Strategy by which a product is distributed through as many channels and channel members as possible.

<u>Exclusive</u> <u>distribution</u> - Strategy by which a manufacturer grants exclusive rights to distribute or sell a product to a limited number of wholesalers or retailers in a given geographic area.

<u>Selective</u> <u>distribution</u> - Strategy by which a company uses only wholesalers and retailers who give special attention to specific products.

<u>Channel</u> <u>conflict</u> - Conflict arising when the members of a distribution channel disagree over the roles they should play or the rewards they should receive.

<u>Channel</u> <u>captain</u> - Channel member who is most powerful in determining the roles and rewards of other members.

<u>Vertical</u> <u>marketing</u> <u>system</u> <u>(VMS)</u> - Unified distribution channel composed of separate businesses centrally controlled by a single member.

<u>Merchant</u> <u>wholesaler</u> - Independent wholesaler who takes legal possession of goods purchased by a variety of manufacturers and then resells them to other businesses.

Full-service merchant wholesaler - Merchant wholesaler who provides credit, marketing, and merchandising services in addition to traditional buying-and-selling services.

Limited-function merchant wholesaler - Merchant wholesaler who provides a limited range of services.

Rack jobber - A full-service merchant wholesaler who sets up displays, tracks inventories, and shelves products for consumer convenience in retail outlets.

Drop shipper - Limited function merchant wholesaler who receives customer orders, negotiates with producers, takes title to goods, and arranges for shipment to customers.

Department store - Large product-line retailer characterized by organization into specialized departments.

Supermarket - Large product-line retailer offering a variety of food and food-related items in specialized departments.

Hypermarket - Very large product-line retailer carrying a wide variety of unrelated products.

Scrambled merchandise - Retail practice of carrying any product that is expected to sell regardless of a store's original product offering.

Specialty store - Small retail store carrying one product line or category of related products.

Bargain retailer - Retailer carrying a wide range of products at bargain prices.

Discount house - Bargain retailer that generates large sales volume by offering goods at substantial price reductions.

Off-price store - Bargain retailer that buys excess inventories from high-quality manufacturers and sells them at discounted prices.

Catalog showroom - Bargain retailer in which customers place orders for catalog items to be picked up at on-premises warehouses.

Factory outlet - Bargain retailer owned by the manufacturer whose products it sells.

Warehouse club (or wholesale club) - Bargain retailer that offers large discounts on brand-name merchandise to customers who have paid annual membership fees.

Convenience store - Retail store offering easy accessibility, extended hours, and fast service.

Direct-response retailing - Nonstore retailing by direct interaction with customers to inform them of products and to receive sales orders.

Mail order (or catalog marketing) - Form of nonstore retailing in which customers place orders for merchandise shown in the catalog and received through the mail.

Video marketing - Nonstore retailing to consumers via standard and cable television.

Telemarketing - Nonstore retailing in which the telephone is used to sell directly to consumers.

Electronic shopping - Nonstore retailing in which information about the seller's products and services is connected into consumers' computers, allowing consumers to receive the information and purchase products in the home.

Direct selling - Form of nonstore retailing typified by door-to-door sales.

Physical distribution - Activities needed to move a product efficiently from manufacturer to consumer.

Warehousing - Physical distribution operation concerned with the storage of goods.

Private warehouse - Warehouse owned by and providing storage for a single company.

Public warehouse - Independently owned and operated warehouse that stores goods for many firms.

Storage warehouse - Warehouse that provides storage for extended periods of time.

Distribution center - Warehouse that provides short-term storage of goods for which demand is both constant and high.

Inventory control - Warehouse operation that tracks inventory on hand and ensures that an adequate supply is in stock at all times.

Materials handling - Warehouse operation that involves the transportation, arrangement, and orderly retrieval of goods in inventory.

Intermodal transportation - Combined use of several different modes of transportation.

Containerization - Transportation method in which goods are sealed in containers at shipping sources and opened when they reach final destinations.

Common carrier - Transporting company, such as a truck line or railroad, that transports goods for any shipper.

Freight forwarder - Transporting company that leases bulk space from other carriers to be resold to firms making smaller shipments.

Contract carrier - Independent transporting company that usually owns the vehicles in which it transports products.

Private carrier - Manufacturer or retailer that maintains its own transportation system.

TRUE-FALSE QUESTIONS

1. The term distribution mix refers to poorly coordinated transportation networks that become "entangled" with one another, thus delaying delivery of the product.

2. Once we called them middlemen, but now we refer to them as intermediaries.

3. Intermediaries are generally classified as wholesalers or retailers.

4. A distribution channel is the path that a product follows from producer to end user.

5. Although once the case, there are no longer any distribution channels that go directly from the producer to the consumer.

6. Intensive distribution entails a producer selecting only wholesalers and retailers who will give the product special attention in sales effort, display advantage, etc.

7. Channel conflict occurs when members of the channel disagree over the roles they should play or the rewards they should receive.

8. In a corporate vertical marketing system (VMS), all stages in the channel are under single ownership.

9. A rack jobber is a limited-function merchant wholesaler.

10. Despite the misleading name, scrambled merchandise means arranging for public display in a store only those products that are very similar and faithful to a store's original product offering.

MULTIPLE CHOICE QUESTIONS

1. Pick the best completion to the following sentence: The more members (or intermediaries) in the channel, then--

   a. the faster shipments will move
   b. the higher the price
   c. the more customers
   d. the less need for advertising

2. Which one of the following is NOT a distribution strategy discussed in the textbook?

   a. intensive distribution
   b. extensive distribution
   c. exclusive distribution
   d. selective distribution

3. It entails distributing a product through as many channels and channel members as possible. What is it?

   a. intensive distribution
   b. extensive distribution
   c. exclusive distribution
   d. selective distribution

4. The textbook says that "Rolex watches, for example, are sold only in selected jewelry stores." This is an illustration of which one of the following?

   a. intensive distribution
   b. extensive distribution
   c. exclusive distribution
   d. selective distribution

5. Listed below are the three types of vertical marketing system (VMS) along with an impostor. Please indicate the item that is out of place in this list.

   a. corporate VMS
   b. contractual VMS
   c. administered VMS
   d. independent VMS

6. In which of the vertical marketing systems (VMS) do we find that channel members are less formally coordinated?

   a. corporate VMS
   b. contractual VMS
   c. administered VMS
   d. independent VMS

7. One of the following attributes is NOT characteristic of a drop shipper. Which is it?

   a. carries inventory
   b. receives orders from customers
   c. negotiates with producer to supply goods
   d. does not handle the product

8. One of the following attributes is NOT characteristic of a rack jobber. Which is it?

   a. sets up display racks
   b. checks inventories
   c. marks prices
   d. markets goods to wholesalers

9. Retail stores in the United States fall into two categories. These categories are--

   a. large and small
   b. product-line and bargain
   c. local and regional
   d. bargain and premium

10. One of the retail establishments shown below is definitely out of place. Which one is it?

   a. discount house
   b. department store
   c. supermarket
   d. hypermarket

11. One of the retail establishments shown below is definitely out of place. Which one is it?

   a. discount house
   b. department store
   c. factory outlet
   d. warehouse club

12. From the point of view of price level, one of the following establishments is out of place in this list. Which is the inappropriate item?

   a. convenience stores
   b. warehouse clubs
   c. wholesale clubs
   d. factory outlets

13. Texaco estimates that in some locations its gasoline sales have increased by about 30 percent. This is credited to--

   a. better gasoline compounds
   b. "pinpoint" advertising
   c. convenience stores
   d. wholesale clubs

14. They buy the excess inventories of well-recognized high-quality manufacturers and sell them at prices up to 60 percent off regular department store prices. What are they?

   a. discount houses
   b. warehouse clubs
   c. off-price stores
   d. catalog showrooms

15. It is effective because it targets specific audiences that have been identified from research lists as likely to be interested in specific products. What is it?

- a. direct mail
- b. telemarketing
- c. express mail
- d. warehouse retailing

16. A Tupperware party would fit into which of the following categories?

- a. electronic shopping
- b. direct mail
- c. direct selling
- d. post-telemarketing

17. If we are referring to the many and varied activities needed to move products efficiently from manufacturer to consumer, then the overall term that we use is--

- a. movement
- b. transportation
- c. tariffing
- d. physical distribution

18. General Electric's Louisville warehouse receives a shipment of 56 refrigerators in one giant container. This makes handling easier and reduces theft and damage. This approach is called--

- a. containerization
- b. counter-individuality
- c. unitization
- d. "transportaining"

19. Several major categories of transportation are treated by the textbook, all the way from pipelines to airplanes. Differences in cost among these methods are most directly related to--

- a. difficulty the load causes the transport agency
- b. delivery speed
- c. nature of the product
- d. season of the year

20. Of all transport modes, the least expensive is--

- a. water
- b. air
- c. rail
- d. pipelines

WRITING TO LEARN

1. Think of as many direct channels of distribution as you possibly can and list them, with an explanation of each. What has happened to the intermediary in such channels?

2. React to this old statement: "You can eliminate the middleman (intermediary), but you cannot eliminate his function."

3. What is meant by the term "intensive distribution"? When should this approach be utilized? Provide illustrations of such uses.

4. Define the role of the channel captain and explain how an individual or firm ends up in that position. Does size of an enterprise become involved in the developing of a channel captain?

5. There are three kinds of vertical marketing system (VMS). Define each, and then go on to show how they differ from one another. Which of the three is the least formal?

6. Tell everything you can about a rack jobber. If you can recall seeing one in action in a large supermarket, tell what he or she was doing. What time of day was it?

7. Although listed as a bargain retailer, the convenience store does not truly fit this category for one very good reason. Provide that reason, and then give personal experiences with this reason.

8. Fully divulge your reaction as a consumer to telemarketing. Is this a successful method for selling merchandise? Why or why not?

9. Provide a brief description of how each of the major modes of transportation provides its own distinctive contributions to marketing. Be sure to include an indication as to the cheapest form as well as the most expensive form.

DISCUSSION OF BUSINESS CASE 15

For purposes of instructional clarity, this chapter on distributing goods and services has had to present certain basic information somewhat in a vacuum. That is to say that to make things understandable, it is necessary to provide explanations as if there were no competition, as if a given firm is operating in total isolation from the rest of the world. Wisely, the text has provided in Business Case 15 a strong testimonial to the fact that you must always plan on the presence of competitors--whether they are there or not! Sadly, the one way to lock out competitors is to engage in a business that causes you to lose money every year. That being the case, no other firm wants to join your industry in losing money. However, as is more often the case, when you stumble upon a tremendous new idea and it goes over fabulously with consumers, then you can be sure that competitors will soon be seen coming over the hill headed for your picnic! We get the impression that Price Club existed for a long time before it considered the fact that rivals would be arriving on the scene. By the time the rivals showed up in force, it was almost too late for Price Club to make any adjustments. Then, if Price Club did adjust, such moves were often seen as nothing more than reactions to the competition and not as innovative steps. What this story could be saying to any business is: "The very moment that you get started, you must begin thinking about how competition will impact your firm. You must make plans right from the very beginning to counterattack with exciting new initiatives of your own." There are so many available techniques for nurturing loyalty among your customers. Failure to put such strategies into practice can lead to the fate of Price Club: loss of your individual corporate identity by merging with a competitor. Getting back to the point of the chapter, being prepared for competition certainly entails readiness to revamp distribution systems so that those systems will help you in the battle for customers.

1. What do you find in the early history of Price Club that could have been changed to make the firm better able to withstand the arrival of competition?

2. Do you feel that Price Club's array of products was too small for major permanent impact? Why or why not?

3. React to this statement: "When competition comes, our best strategy is to do even better exactly what we are doing now."

4. What do you think of this creative idea? Price Club could have withdrawn from retailing and become a wholesaler servicing as its clients all of its previous competitors!

ANSWERS TO TRUE-FALSE QUESTIONS

1. F (p. 367)
2. T (p. 367)
3. T (p. 367)
4. T (p. 368)
5. F (p. 368)
6. F (p. 371)
7. T (p. 372)
8. T (p. 374)
9. F (p. 374)
10. F (p. 376)

ANSWERS TO MULTIPLE CHOICE QUESTIONS

1. b (p. 369)
2. b (p. 371)
3. a (p. 371)
4. c (p. 371)
5. d (p. 374)
6. d (p. 374)
7. a (p. 374)
8. d (p. 374)
9. b (p. 376)
10. a (p. 376)
11. b (p. 377)
12. a (p. 379)
13. c (p. 379)
14. c (p. 377)
15. a (p. 380)
16. c (p. 382)
17. d (p. 382)
18. c (p. 383)
19. b (p. 383)
20. a (p. 385)

CHAPTER SIXTEEN

UNDERSTANDING MONEY AND BANKING

CHAPTER OVERVIEW

Just about any object can serve as money if it meets four criteria: it must be portable, divisible, durable, and stable. In broad terms, money serves three functions: medium of exchange, store of value, and unit of account. The M1 money supply consists of currency, demand deposits, and other "checkable" deposits. The use of credit cards has become so widespread that many people refer to them as "plastic money." The major types of financial institutions are commercial banks, savings and loan associations, mutual savings banks, credit unions, and insurance companies. Individual retirement accounts (IRAs) are pension funds that wage earners and their spouses can set up to supplement other retirement funds. Many commercial banks offer trust services--the management of funds left in the bank's trust. The three international services offered by banks are currency exchange, letters of credit, and banker's acceptances. The Federal Reserve System, the Comptroller of the Currency, and the Federal Deposit Insurance Corporation are all involved in regulating commercial banks. "The Fed" serves as the government's bank, as the bankers' bank, oversees the banking community, and controls the money supply. Monetary policy tools of the Fed are reserve requirements, discount-rate controls, open-market operations, and selected credit controls.

LEARNING OBJECTIVES

1. Define money and identify the different forms that it takes in the nation's money supply.

2. Describe the different kinds of financial institutions that make up the U.S. financial system and explain the services they offer.

3. Explain how banks create money and identify the means by which they are regulated.

4. Discuss the functions of the Federal Reserve System and describe the tools it uses to control the money supply.

5. Identify five important ways in which the financial industry is changing.

DISCUSSION OF OPENING VIGNETTE

In the chapters just previous to this one, you have been reading about the various aspects of marketing. You will recall the terms "target market" and "market segmentation." These terms emphasize that it is important to make specific decisions concerning just whom you will serve with your product or service. Once you know who is out there waiting for you, your firm can more effectively operate in such a way as to make that particular segment happy. Implicit in all this talk of locating your potential audience is this statement: Be sure that you have the means to effectively meet the wants and needs of your market segment. Now, this is where First Interstate Bancorporation ran into trouble. The narrative leads us to believe that they were not equipped to be big-time operators in international circles. What's the old saying? "When you play with the big kids, you can get hurt!" But perhaps playing out of their league is not the whole story of First Interstate. The narrative indicates clearly that the bank was not even doing a good job in that portion of its operation that catered to the lightly-funded ordinary borrowing citizen. Here's a key sentence that tells what Edward M. Carson began to demand of his bank officers: "One strategy called for identifying bad risks before they went on the books rather than after." Actually, such a strategy is no cutting-edge breakthrough that has come with our technologically-sophisticated age. Even the earliest bankers knew this rule. Sadly though, First Interstate loan officers had not been applying it. No one is saying that a loan officer must be able to use a crystal ball and thus predict who is a good risk and who is not. But we can say that a sharp loan officer has many other devices for making a very intelligent guess as to which customer is a good risk and which one is not. So, when Edward M. Carson had First Interstate getting down to the basics of good banking again, the picture began to improve immeasurably.

1. Which do you feel was the _major_ problem at First Interstate Bancorporation as Edward M. Carson came aboard? Why?

2. Evaluate this statement: "A bank is in business to lend money. We can't afford to be too snooty when someone comes in to borrow money!"

3. Some people have (rightly or wrongly) credited Mark Twain with saying: "I'm not so concerned with return _on_ my money, but rather with return _of_ my money." How relevant was this statement at First Interstate before Mr. Carson came along.

4. What do you think of Mr. Carson having First Interstate employees standing on the sidewalk in front of Security Pacific Bank handing out coupons?

ANNOTATED KEY TERMS

Money - Any object which is portable, divisible, durable, and stable and serves as a medium of exchange, a store of value, and a unit of account.

M-1 - Measure of the money supply that includes only the most liquid (spendable) forms of money.

Currency - Government-issued paper money and metal coins.

Check - Demand-deposit order instructing a bank to pay a given sum to a specified "payee."

Demand deposit - Bank account funds that may be withdrawn at any time.

M-2 - Measure of the money supply that includes all the components of M-1 plus the forms of money that can be easily converted into spendable form.

Time deposit - Bank funds that cannot be withdrawn without notice or transferred by check.

Money market mutual fund - Fund of short-term, low-risk financial securities purchased with the assets of investor-owners pooled by a non-bank institution.

Commercial bank - Federal- or state-chartered financial institution accepting deposits that it uses to make loans and to earn profits.

State bank - Commercial bank chartered by an individual state.

National bank - Commercial bank chartered by the federal government.

Prime rate - Interest rate available to a bank's most creditworthy customers.

Savings and loan association (S&L) - Financial institution accepting deposits and making loans primarily for home mortgages.

Mutual savings bank - Financial institution whose depositors are owners sharing in its profits.

Credit union - Financial institution that accepts deposits from, and makes loans to, only its members, usually employees of a particular organization.

Pension fund - Nondeposit pool of funds managed to provide retirement income for its members.

Insurance company - Nondeposit institution that invests funds collected as premiums charged for insurance coverage.

Finance company - Nondeposit institution that specializes in making loans to businesses and consumers.

Securities investment dealer (broker) - Nondeposit institution that buys and sells stocks and bonds both for investors and for its own accounts.

Investment banker - Financial intermediary that matches buyers and sellers of newly issued securities.

Individual retirement account (IRA) - Tax-deferred pension fund with which wage earners supplement other retirement funds.

Keogh plan - Tax-deferred pension plan for the self-employed.

Trust services - Bank management of an individual's investments, payments, or estate.

Letter of credit - Bank promise, issued for a buyer, to pay a designated firm a certain amount of money if specified conditions are met.

Banker's acceptance - Bank promise, issued for a buyer, to pay a designated firm a specified amount at a future date.

Automated teller machine (ATM) - Electronic machine that allows customers to conduct account-related activities 24 hours a day, seven days a week.

Electronic funds transfer (EFT) - Communication of fund transfer information over wire, cable, or microwave.

Federal Deposit Insurance Corporation (FDIC) - Federal agency that guarantees the safety of all deposits up to $100,000 in the financial institutions that it insures.

Financial Institutions Reform, Recovery, and Enforcement Act (FIRREA) - Federal law (1989) establishing new regulations and regulatory bodies to oversee the thrift industry.

Office of Thrift Supervision (OTS) - Federal agency that regulates thrift institutions belonging to the Savings and Loan Association Insurance Fund.

Resolution Trust Corporation (RTC) - Federal agency set up to resolve all troubled thrift cases occurring between January 1989 and August 1992.

Federal Reserve System (the Fed) - The central bank of the United States, which acts as the government's bank, services member commercial banks, and controls the nation's money supply.

Float - Total amount of checks written but not yet cleared through Federal Reserve.

Monetary policy - Policies by which the Federal Reserve manages the nation's money supply and interest rates.

Reserve requirement - Percentage of its deposits that a bank must hold in cash or on deposit with a Federal Reserve Bank.

Discount rate - Interest rate at which member banks can borrow money from the Federal Reserve.

Open-market operations - The Federal Reserve's sales and purchases of securities in the open market.

Selective credit controls - Federal Reserve's authority to set both margin requirements for consumer stock purchases and credit rules for other consumer purchases.

Debit card - Plastic card that allows an individual to transfer money between accounts.

Point-of-sale (POS) terminal - Electronic device that allows customers to pay for retail purchases with debit cards.

Financial supermarket - Nonbank firm that offers a broad array of financial services.

TRUE-FALSE QUESTIONS

1. Contrary to many misconceptions on the matter, money does not have to be portable.

2. An important function of money is as a store of value.

3. As a rule, checking accounts are NOT included in the M-1 money supply.

4. As a rule, time deposits are NOT included in the M-1 money supply.

5. To remain competitive, U.S. banks now offer some commercial loans at rates below the prime rate.

6. Insurance companies collect large pools of funds from the premiums charged for coverage. Funds are invested in stocks, real estate, and other assets.

7. IRAs are pension funds that wage earners and their spouses can set up to supplement other retirement funds.

8. Taxes on Keogh plans are always deferred until earners withdraw funds.

9. As might be expected, there are no state-chartered banks that are members of the Federal Reserve System.

10. Unlike credit cards, debit cards cannot be used to make retail purchases.

MULTIPLE CHOICE QUESTIONS

1. The textbook offers the four criteria any object must meet if it is to serve as money. Three of the criteria have been listed below, along with an out-of-place item. Please select the inappropriate item.

   a. printability
   b. portability
   c. durability
   d. stability

2. Which one of the following is a function of money?

   a. ability to barter
   b. investment inventory
   c. store of value
   d. medium of recount

3. One of the following elements is a part of the M-2 money supply. Which one is it?

   a. currency
   b. demand deposits
   c. time deposits
   d. "checkable" accounts

4. The textbook says that there are over 111 million U.S. credit card holders. The total number of cards these people hold is--

   a. 111 million
   b. 457 million
   c. 750 million
   d. 1 billion

5. Which figure below best indicates the number of commercial banks in the United States today?

   a. 5,000
   b. 12,000
   c. 50,000
   d. 98,000

6. Which figure below best indicates the number of credit unions in the United States today?

   a. 13,000
   b. 17,000
   c. 21,500
   d. 27,650

7. They can be opened only by self-employed people--doctors, small business owners, and consultants (as a few examples). Taxes on them can be deferred until earners withdraw funds. What are they?

   a. IRAs
   b. tax on residual title (TORT) funds
   c. Keogh plans
   d. credit union accounts

8. There are three main international services offered by banks. Which one of the following is NOT one of these three services?

   a. currency exchange
   b. letters of credit
   c. banker's acceptance
   d. offshore account checking

9. Electronic funds transfer (EFT) systems transfer many kinds of financial information via electrical impulses over wire, cable, or microwave. The most popular form of EFT is the--

    a. float
    b. ATM
    c. banker's acceptance
    d. letter of credit

10. By taking in deposits and then making loans, commercial banks can have which of the following effects on the nation's money supply?

    a. decrease the money supply
    b. expand the money supply
    c. make no change in the money supply
    d. jeopardize the money supply

11. According to critics, deregulation of the savings and loan institutions had which of the following effects on the bankers involved?

    a. made them more hesitant to provide funds for consumers
    b. turned their eyes toward the stock market
    c. made them leave the S&L industry in great numbers
    d. gave them new incentives for making risky investments

12. In the story of the "S&L collapse," which of the following events came first chronologically?

    a. junk-bond prices took a nosedive
    b. oil prices plummeted
    c. recession in the agricultural heartland
    d. recession went national

13. Which of the following abolished the Federal Home Loan Bank Board and the Federal Savings and Loan Insurance Corporation?

    a. FIRREA
    b. OTS
    c. RTC
    d. ALICIA

14. Under FDIC supervision, this institution manages thrifts in immediate danger of failure, approves mergers between failed and healthy institutions, liquidates some troubled thrifts, and disposes of some assets. What is this institution?

    a. RTC
    b. ALICIA
    c. OTS
    d. FIRREA

15. Which one of the following is NOT listed as a function of the Federal Reserve System of the United States?

   a. deciding how many bills (of the currency) to destroy
   b. deciding how many bills (of the currency) to produce
   c. lending money to the government
   d. cooperative regulation of banks with Canadian "Fed"

16. Which one of the following is the best illustration of a characteristic of inflation?

   a. demand for goods and services decreases
   b. money supply grows too large
   c. Fed pulls more surprise inspections of banks
   d. oil supplies are depleted

17. Which one of the following is a tool used by the Fed for controlling the money supply?

   a. selective credit controls
   b. accelerated check processing
   c. limit on number of new checking accounts
   d. "meltdown" of certain Federal Reserve Banks

18. Which one of the following is NOT a tool used by the Fed for controlling the money supply?

   a. reserve requirements
   b. discount-rate controls
   c. open-market operations
   d. denied franking privileges

19. Which of the following actions by the Fed is most likely to *decrease* the money supply?

   a. the Fed buys bonds
   b. the Fed lowers the discount rate
   c. the Fed raises the reserve requirements
   d. the Fed lowers the margin requirement

20. Which of the following phrases is most characteristic of the debit card?

   a. does not increase funds at an individual's disposal
   b. same as a credit card
   c. cannot be used to make retail purchases
   d. does more than just allow transfer of money between accounts

WRITING TO LEARN

1. Consider the four criteria that must be met for an object to be considered as money. Then, write an explanation of each, employing a liberal use of illustrations. Pay particular attention to "stability."

2. Since you have already had the chapter on accounting, you are now in a position to relate that chapter to the money function known as "unit of account." Do so. Also, indicate that it is a shame that accounting cannot deal with anything that cannot be given a monetary value.

3. Explain the difference between a demand deposit and a time deposit. Then, calling upon your own experiences, relate how the differences between the two are becoming blurred.

4. What are the differences between a credit card and a debit card? Do you feel that the debit card is indeed the way of the future? Why or why not?

5. Write a very short historical sketch of the savings and loan collapse. Be sure to treat the four key phases alluded to by the textbook.

6. Explain what a credit union is. What are some of the main ways in which a credit union differs from a commercial bank?

7. Explain the process by which commercial banks can expand the nation's money supply.

8. List the four main tools used by the Fed in controlling the nation's money supply and tell how each one works. Pay particular attention to the Fed's buying and selling of U.S. Treasury bonds.

9. Explain the purpose and the many results that have flowed from the passage of the Financial Institutions Reform, Recovery, and Enforcement Act (FIRREA). Be sure to indicate the government institutions that have disappeared under FIRREA.

DISCUSSION OF BUSINESS CASE 16

Many of us are bombarded with opportunities to acquire a credit card. Each card seems to offer the ideal situation: low annual interest rate, little or no annual fee, frequent bonuses for this and that, special deals at motels, airlines, fast-food restaurants, etc. Since we know that the bottom line is going to be much the same with all of these cards, there is a temptation to throw away literature on a new credit card. And, most assuredly, many people disregarded the chance at the new GM MasterCard. On the other hand, the card was perfectly in tune with some people's desires. Listen to these fabulous results! "Within the first three months of operation, the GM MasterCard attracted over $2 billion in new balances and 3 million accounts." Hopefully, the mind at GM that thought up the idea was rewarded for his or her contribution to GM success. No doubt about it, substantial savings will be enjoyed by those persons who fit the GM MasterCard combination of GM, MCI, Marriott, Avis, and Mobil. Trouble is that many people who take the GM card may be customers of AT&T, Holiday Inn, Hertz, and Texaco. Card holders will have to work out such matters themselves. Did you notice that credit card companies do not compete on interest rates? Such competition could lead to a "ruinous price war." Remember in a previous chapter you read that in an oligopoly the small number of firms do not compete on price, but rather on non-price issues? Well, the same is true for the institutions issuing credit cards. They will compete with all sorts of "gimmicks," but they will all essentially stay pretty close to one another on that interest rate charged. As the narrative was telling that to us, it may very well have been hinting that the non-interest features of one card will about equal those of any other card. But, so far as we know, the GM MasterCard is the only one offering a favorable car purchase as part of the deal!

1. How do you account for the significant success of the GM MasterCard? Is the entire secret to be found in the connection between the card and a GM car? Why or why not?

2. Do you feel that Procter & Gamble would have the same success with a credit card that allowed cut-rate purchase of that firm's products? Explain.

3. To sign up more GM cardholders, would GM be wise to drastically reduce the interest charges on its card? Explain the positive and negative aspects of such a move.

4. Evaluate this statement: "A car company has no business getting into banking. They don't understand finance and they may be making a big mistake."

ANSWERS TO TRUE-FALSE QUESTIONS

1. F (p. 396)
2. T (p. 396)
3. F (p. 397)
4. T (p. 397)
5. T (p. 401)
6. T (p. 401)
7. T (p. 403)
8. T (p. 403)
9. F (p. 408-409)
10. F (p. 414)

ANSWERS TO MULTIPLE CHOICE QUESTIONS

1. a (p. 396)
2. c (p. 396)
3. c (p. 397-398)
4. d (p. 399)
5. b (p. 400)
6. a (p. 401)
7. c (p. 403)
8. d (p. 403)
9. b (p. 405)
10. b (p. 406)
11. d (p. 407)
12. c (p. 407)
13. a (p. 408)
14. a (p. 408)
15. d (p. 409)
16. b (p. 410)
17. a (p. 411)
18. d (p. 411)
19. c (p. 412)
20. a (p. 414)

CHAPTER SEVENTEEN

MANAGING FINANCE, RISK, AND INSURANCE

CHAPTER OVERVIEW

The business activity known as finance (or corporate finance) typically entails three responsibilities: determining a firm's long-term investments; obtaining funds to pay for those investments; and conducting the firm's everyday financial activities. Financial managers plan and control the acquisition and dispersal of a firm's financial resources. To manage short-term expenditures, financial managers must pay special attention to accounts payable, accounts receivable, and inventories. Sources of short-term funds are trade credit, secured and unsecured loans, commercial paper, and factoring accounts receivable. Sources of long-term funds are debt financing (long-term loans and corporate bonds) and equity financing (common stock and retained earnings). Preferred stock is referred to as "hybrid" because it has some of the features of both corporate bonds and common stocks. Speculative risks involve the possibility of loss or gain. Pure risks involve only the possibility of loss or no loss. Some methods for handling risk are risk avoidance, risk control, risk retention, and risk transfer. In risk transfer, the risk is shifted to another company--an insurance company. There are two kinds of private insurers: stock insurance companies and mutual insurance companies.

LEARNING OBJECTIVES

1. Describe the responsibilities of a financial manager.

2. Identify four sources of short-term financing for businesses.

3. Distinguish between the various sources of long-term financing and explain the risks entailed by each type.

4. Show how financial returns to investors are related to the risks they take.

5. Explain how risk affects business operations and identify the five steps in the risk-management process.

6. Describe the basic workings of the insurance industry and explain how insurers make profits.

7. Distinguish among the different types of business insurance.

DISCUSSION OF OPENING VIGNETTE

Let's engage in a little entrepreneurial philosophy. This may come as a shock to you. If you pursue a business major, you will probably never be taught anything about a business. Sounds strange, doesn't it? You will learn invaluable things about how to run a business and how to keep track of what is happening to your firm. But you will not be taught a business, such as furniture, car rental, groceries, curtains, swimwear, agriculture, entertainment, kitchen appliances, broadcasting, etc. Some new business graduates may be tempted to assume they can start ANY business and succeed because they have had training in how to run a business. Such a graduate had better not open a furniture store unless that graduate fully understands: headboards, mattresses, sturdy wood construction, china cabinets, cedar chests, etc. Notice, this is basically what H. Ross Perot was saying to McCurry and Kusin, advising them to keep "learning the business and market inside out." To do this best, Perot advised that the two entrepreneurs "open a single store and run it themselves." That was the way that the two would fully absorb all there was to know about computer software. There is also the other important lesson about Babbage's. You first encountered the lesson in a previous chapter on starting a small business. One of the reasons why some new small firms fail is because they are undercapitalized. Failure is exactly what would have happened to Babbage's if H. Ross Perot had not come along. We might make up the following rule for new business ventures. "Part One: Determine the amount of reserve cash you will need to start up the business. Part Two: Take the figure you arrived at in Part One and multiply it by five! Part Three: Don't open for business until you have acquired this latter figure." McCurry and Kusin were fortunate that H. Ross Perot arrived on the scene. Not only was his money welcome, but McCurry and Kusin knew Perot's advice was coming from the lips of a man who knew what he was talking about!

1. In the entire tale of Babbage's, which was the most serious problem the two partners faced? Explain why.

2. What are some very good reasons why McCurry and Kusin did not have sufficient funds at the beginning of Babbage's?

3. Evaluate and amplify this statement: "H. Ross Perot had money, was an astute businessman, but he also knew the field into which McCurry and Kusin were entering."

4. What might be some signs that McCurry and Kusin were in a position to open a second Babbage's store?

ANNOTATED KEY TERMS

Finance (or corporate finance) - Activities concerned with determining a firm's long-term investments, obtaining the funds to pay for them, and conducting its everyday financial activities.

Financial manager - Manager responsible for planning and controlling the acquisition and dispersal of a firm's financial resources.

Cash-flow management - Management of cash inflows and outflows to ensure adequate funds for purchases and the productive use of excess funds.

Financial plan - A firm's strategies for reaching some future financial position.

Inventory - Materials and goods which are held by a company but which will be sold within the year.

Trade credit - Granting of credit by one firm to another.

Open-book credit - Form of trade credit in which sellers ship merchandise on faith that payment will be forthcoming.

Promissory note - Form of trade credit in which buyers sign promise-to-pay agreements before merchandise is shipped.

Trade draft - Form of trade credit in which buyers must sign statements of payment terms attached to the merchandise by sellers.

Trade acceptance - Trade draft that has been signed by the buyer.

Secured loan - Loan for which the borrower must provide collateral.

Collateral - Asset pledged by borrowers that may be seized by lenders in case of nonpayment.

Pledging accounts receivable - Using accounts receivable as loan collateral.

Unsecured loan - Loan for which collateral is not required.

Line of credit - Standing arrangement in which a lender agrees to make available a specified amount of funds upon the borrower's request.

Revolving credit agreement - Arrangement in which a lender agrees to make funds available on a continuing basis.

Commercial paper - Short-term securities, or notes, containing a borrower's promise to pay.

Debt financing - Long-term borrowing from sources outside a company.

Corporate bond - Contract in which the issuer promises to pay holders a certain amount of money on a specified date.

Bond indenture - Statement of the terms of a corporate bond.

Equity financing - Use of common stock or retained earnings to raise long-term funding.

Venture capital - Outside equity financing provided in return for part ownership of the borrowing firm.

Capital structure - Relative mix of a firm's debt and equity financing.

Risk-return relationship - Principle that although safer investments tend to offer lower returns, riskier investments tend to offer higher returns.

Risk - Uncertainty about future events.

Speculative risk - Risk involving the possibility of gain or loss.

Pure risk - Risk involving only the possibility of loss or no loss.

Risk management - Process of conserving a firm's earning power and assets by reducing the threat of losses due to uncontrollable events.

Risk avoidance - Practice of avoiding risk by declining or ceasing to participate in an activity.

Risk control - Practice of minimizing the frequency or severity of losses from risky activities.

Risk retention - Practice of covering a firm's losses with its own funds.

Risk transfer - Practice of transferring a firm's risk to another firm.

Premium - Fee paid by a policyholder for insurance coverage.

Insurance policy - Formal agreement in which an insurer promises to pay a policyholder a specified amount in the event of certain losses.

Deductible - Agreed-upon amount of loss that an insured party absorbs prior to reimbursement from an insurer.

Stock insurance company - Private insurer that sells its stock to the public.

Mutual insurance company - Private insurer owned by its policyholders.

Liability insurance - Insurance covering losses resulting from damage to people or property when the insured is judged responsible.

Workers' compensation coverage - Coverage provided by a firm to employees for medical expenses, loss of wages, and rehabilitation costs resulting from job-related injuries or disease.

Property insurance - Insurance covering losses resulting from physical damage to or loss of the insured's real estate or personal property.

Business interruption insurance - Insurance covering income lost during times when a company is unable to conduct business.

Life insurance - Insurance paying benefits to the policyholder's survivors.

Group life insurance - Insurance underwritten for a group as a whole rather than for each individual in it.

Health insurance - Insurance covering losses resulting from medical and hospital expenses as well as income lost from injury or disease.

Disability income insurance - Insurance providing continuous income when disability keeps the insured from gainful employment.

Employee leasing - Obtaining employee services from personnel services instead of hiring permanent employees.

Health-care coalition - Group of companies joined together to obtain more cost-effective programs for themselves and their employees.

TRUE-FALSE QUESTIONS

1. Financial managers plan and control the acquisition and dispersal of a firm's financial resources.

2. To manage short-term expenditures, financial managers must pay special attention to accounts payable, accounts receivable, and inventories.

3. To manage short-term expenditures, financial managers must pay special attention to fixed assets, stockholders' equity, and retained earnings.

4. Accounts receivable consist of funds due from customers who have bought on credit.

5. Trade credit is defined as a long-term loan from one firm to another.

6. Pledging accounts receivable occurs when a customer "pledges" to pay for his or her credit purchases within sixty days of acquiring goods from a firm.

7. Because it is backed solely by the issuing firm's promise to pay, commercial paper is an option for only the largest and most creditworthy firms.

8. Retained earnings are profits of a firm retained for the firm's use rather than paid out in dividends.

9. Wise and experienced investors usually expect large returns for secure investments such as government-insured bonds.

10. When a firm cannot escape or control the potential for large risks, these risks are handed over to an insurance company. This action is known as risk avoidance.

MULTIPLE CHOICE QUESTIONS

1. The business activity known as finance (or corporate finance) typically entails three responsibilities. They are listed below, along with an inappropriate item. Please identify the impostor.

    a. determining a firm's long-term investments
    b. obtaining funds to pay for those investments
    c. conducting the firm's everyday financial activities
    d. recruiting human resources for the finance function

2. Financial managers must ensure that the firm always has enough funds on hand to purchase materials it needs. At the same time, there may be funds that are not needed immediately; these must be invested. All of this activity is covered by the specific term--

   a. financial planning
   b. factoring
   c. pledging
   d. cash-flow management

3. To manage short-term expenditures, financial managers keep a close eye on certain accounts. Which one of the following is NOT one of these accounts?

   a. bonds payable
   b. accounts payable
   c. accounts receivable
   d. inventories

4. For a manufacturing firm, there are three types of inventory. From the list below, select the only item that should be included among these three types.

   a. unaccountable inventory
   b. shipping inventory
   c. work-in-process inventory
   d. secondary inventory

5. Which one of the following is least likely to be a source of short-term funding for a firm?

   a. trade credit
   b. mortgages
   c. commercial paper
   d. pledging accounts receivable

6. "Trade credit" is defined as a short-term loan from one firm to another. In the list below will be found one form of trade credit. Which is it?

   a. trade acceptance
   b. trade center
   c. rebottling
   d. bond issuance

7. When accounts receivable are used as collateral for a short-term loan, the process is called--

   a. factoring
   b. promissory procedure
   c. credit line
   d. pledging

8. Some firms can raise short-term funds by short-term securities, or notes, containing the borrower's promise to pay. It is an option for only the largest and most creditworthy firms. This option is referred to as--

   a. commercial paper
   b. corporate bonds
   c. preferred stock
   d. a proxy

9. It is defined as a contract or it can be defined as a promise to pay the holder a certain amount of money on a specified date in the distant future. Which of the choices below best fits the description you have just read?

   a. commercial paper
   b. corporate bond
   c. promissory note
   d. trade credit

10. The textbook indicates that people who purchase common stock seek profits in two forms. What are these two forms?

   a. profit at purchase, profit at sale
   b. stock splits and freedom from broker fees
   c. dividends and appreciation
   d. common and preferred

11. When a corporate bond is issued, full details of the issue (interest rate, face value, maturity date, etc.) are disclosed in the "contract." This contract printed on the bond is usually referred to as the--

   a. buyer's guide
   b. warranty
   c. debenture
   d. indenture

12. A firm that makes a profit in a given period of operation can do several things with the profit. Some of it can be given out as dividends to the firm's stockholders. Some of it can be kept in the business to help finance operations for the next period. Funds kept for this latter purpose are referred to as--

   a. retained earnings
   b. cash flow
   c. utility net profit
   d. venture capital

13. Many newer businesses--especially those undergoing rapid growth--cannot get funds they need through borrowing alone. They turn to outside equity funding provided in return for part ownership. The appropriate term here is--

    a. retained earnings
    b. cash flow
    c. utility net profit
    d. venture capital

14. One of the forms of financing listed below is often referred to as a "hybrid." Which of the following is it?

    a. common stock
    b. corporate bonds
    c. preferred stock
    d. bank borrowing

15. A firm relies on a mix of debt and equity to raise the cash needed for capital outlays. Of the options below, which is the most appropriate designation for this mix?

    a. marketing mix
    b. debt-to-equity ratio
    c. capital structure
    d. long-term funding

16. Keeping the risk-return relationship in mind, which of the following securities would be expected to at least promise the payment of the highest returns.

    a. extremely secure government bonds
    b. corporate bonds rated high by the rating services
    c. high-rated municipal bonds
    d. junk bonds from firms with uncertain reputations

17. It is defined as conserving the firm's earning power and assets by reducing the threat of losses due to uncontrollable events. What is it?

    a. risk management
    b. financial planning
    c. cash-flow analysis
    d. risk transfer

18. To avoid future liability for difficulties in childbirth, a general practice physician ceases delivering babies. In so doing, that physician is practicing--

    a. risk transfer
    b. risk avoidance
    c. risk control
    d. risk retention

19. Although there are exceptions, an insurable risk must meet four criteria. Of the choices listed below, only one is among the four criteria. Which is it?

    a. must not be random
    b. predictability
    c. within the policyholder's control
    d. cost effective

20. The Blue Corporation has an automatic sprinkler system in its plant, has very strict rules about smoking on company property, conducts weekly training in fire-fighting for its employees, equips each employee station with two fire extinguishers, and keeps the exterior of its building hosed down. The Blue Corporation is practicing--

    a. risk avoidance
    b. risk transfer
    c. risk control
    d. risk retention

WRITING TO LEARN

1. In strictly your own terminology, describe the responsibilities of a financial manager.

2. To stay on top of his or her firm's short-term financing, the financial manager keeps an eye on several accounts. Tell what these accounts are and describe how keeping track of them is so important to the financial manager.

3. Although accounts receivable are nothing more than promises that money will eventually be coming to the firm, explain how accounts receivable can become instrumental in providing a sudden flow of cash.

4. Explain what is meant by the term "trade credit," and then proceed to completely define its most common forms.

5. What is commercial paper? Give a lengthy example of how it operates to provide funds for a firm in need of quick, short-term cash.

6. Commercial paper and corporate bonds are both forms of borrowing. However, some may consider that there is a world of difference between them. Explain that "world of difference."

7. Define business interruption insurance. Then spin your own narrative of a fictional company that finds itself badly in need of such coverage.

8. Furnish as many reasons as you can that will explain why so many writers refer to preferred stock as a "hybrid" security.

9. Expound upon each of the four ways of handling risk. Be sure to provide numerous illustrations of each of the four ways.

DISCUSSION OF BUSINESS CASE 17

When you are deathly sick--or at least think you are--you pay a visit to your doctor and he or she is able to relieve the symptoms. Feeling so very ill, you seem in stark contrast to the healthy and energetic physician attending you. You may be tempted to ask: "Do doctors ever get sick?" Of course they do, and they die of the same causes that plague the rest of us. In similar fashion, we turn our major risks over to an insurance company, and are tempted to ask: "Do insurance companies ever experience risk?" Rest assured that they do. Most, if not all, insurance companies turn to other insurance companies for back-up. In other words, they take some of the risk you transfer to them, and then transfer it to still another company. If an insurance company can develop a good idea of the kind of risk it is facing, it can compensate by charging premiums that will cover the payout of benefits down the line. The insurance company employees who do this sort of calculating are called actuaries. But the UNUM CEO, James F. Orr III, knows that such calculations must be constantly updated, and they can sometimes improperly account for disasters over the horizon. Perhaps the most famous insurance name around the world, Lloyd's of London, has experienced the latter phenomenon over the past several years. In recent memory, Hurricane Hugo, the San Francisco earthquake, the Exxon Valdez oil spill, and the Piper Alpha oil rig tragedy in the North Sea all hit during a relatively short time period. Lloyd's had major exposure in all of these disasters. The resulting claims were so great that many backers of Lloyd's found their investments drastically depleted. Although Lloyd's and its backers were allowing many clients to transfer risks to them, they were unable, in turn, to transfer sufficient risks to some other institution. As James F. Orr III will tell you, insurance companies, too, must learn to successfully cope with their risks.

1. Do you think that James F. Orr III has done a good job of taking a fresh look at his firm's risks? Why or why not?

2. Explain the significance of this statement from the case: "If eight workers out of a thousand should become disabled, however, [the firm] would suffer serious financial losses."

3. With the previous question in mind, tell why you think or do NOT think that running an insurance company is a lot like gambling in a casino.

4. Going back over the narrative, explain why it would make sense to charge higher premiums to California policyholders than to South Dakota policyholders. Why would some consider such an approach unfair?

ANSWERS TO TRUE-FALSE QUESTIONS

1. T (p. 422)
2. T (p. 423)
3. F (p. 423)
4. T (p. 423)
5. F (p. 424)
6. F (p. 425)
7. T (p. 426)
8. T (p. 428-429)
9. F (p. 431-432)
10. F (p. 434)

ANSWERS TO MULTIPLE CHOICE QUESTIONS

1. d (p. 421)
2. d (p. 422)
3. a (p. 423)
4. c (p. 423-424)
5. b (p. 424)
6. a (p. 424)
7. d (p. 425)
8. a (p. 426)
9. b (p. 427)
10. c (p. 428)
11. d (p. 427)
12. a (p. 428-429)
13. d (p. 429)
14. c (p. 430)
15. c (p. 430-431)
16. d (p. 431-432)
17. a (p. 432)
18. b (p. 432, 434)
19. b (p. 435-436)
20. c (p. 432, 434)

CHAPTER EIGHTEEN

UNDERSTANDING SECURITIES MARKETS

CHAPTER OVERVIEW

Stocks and bonds are known as securities because they represent secured, or asset-based, claims on the part of investors. Stockholders have claims on some of the corporation's assets because each share represents part ownership. Bonds, in contrast, represent strictly financial claims for money owed to holders by a company. Stock values are expressed in three different ways: par value, market value, book value. A stock exchange is an organization of individuals formed to provide an institutional setting in which stock can be bought and sold. The largest U.S. stock exchange is the New York Stock Exchange. The over-the-counter (OTC) market is so called because its original traders were somewhat like retailers; they kept supplies of shares on hand and sold them to interested buyers as opportunities arose. Today, the OTC consists of many traders in different locations linked by electronic communications. The U.S. bond market is supplied by three major sources: the U.S. government, municipalities, and corporations. With regard to maturity dates, there are three types of bonds: callable, serial, and convertible. Daily transactions in both stocks and bonds are widely reported. Bull markets are periods of upward-moving stock prices; periods of falling prices are called bear markets.

LEARNING OBJECTIVES

1. Explain the difference between primary and secondary securities markets.

2. Discuss the value of common stock and preferred stock to shareholders and describe the secondary market for each type of security.

3. Distinguish among various types of bonds in terms of their issuers, safety, and retirement.

4. Describe the investment opportunities offered by mutual funds and commodities.

5. Explain the process by which securities are bought and sold.

6. Explain how securities markets are regulated.

DISCUSSION OF OPENING VIGNETTE

Snapple's growth has been absolutely phenomenal. The story illustrates that, despite so many sad stories of new businesses going under, some firms can start small and build in a most inspiring way. Sometimes the results are delightfully shocking even to those persons who had the original faith in the firm. Particularly scintillating has been the firm's performance since the IPO (initial public offering) of its stock. Their story is so much like a fairy tale that we must caution ourselves that a first selling of stock (or "going public") is seldom as spectacular as we have just witnessed in the case of Snapple Beverage Corporation. When a corporation and its investment banker figure that a share of stock will bring in $15 and then some of the shares sell as high as $33.75, this means a tremendous amount of <u>unexpected</u> new capital coming to the firm-- depending upon the arrangement the firm has with its investment banker. Let's deal with some rounded figures without consideration of investment bankers' fees. If a firm such as Snapple planned to sell 5 million shares at $15 per share, that would mean gross proceeds of $75 million. If the stock actually sold for say $30 per share, then we are talking about gross proceeds of $150 million. That's an additional $75 million that the firm had not counted on! How they would wisely make use of this additional capital is a major matter. Maybe such funds should be used to get ready for the big challenge looming up ahead. If indeed Coke and Pepsi enter the New Age, natural-flavor, health-conscious drink market, there can be tough competition. The ability of Coke and Pepsi to market a product on an international scale is awesome. In the worst case scenario for Snapple, Coke and Pepsi will come in and dominate the New Age market, and then offer to buy out Snapple. Knowing such things are possible and being sharp operators, the Snapple team is probably fully prepared for the big battle.

1. Do you feel that Coke and/or Pepsi will be able to establish themselves as the leaders in the New Age drink market? Why or why not?

2. How do you account for the popularity of Snapple Beverage Corporation among stock investors?

3. The case narrative points out that marketing of Snapple has been handled very well. Tell why you agree or disagree with such a statement.

4. If you were the management of Snapple and you discovered you had an extra $75 million, how would you spend it for the firm?

ANNOTATED KEY TERMS

Securities - Stocks and bonds representing secured, or asset-based, claims by investors against issuers.

Primary securities market - Market in which new stocks and bonds are traded.

Investment banker - Financial institution engaged in purchasing and reselling new securities.

Secondary securities market - Market in which existing stocks and bonds are traded.

Par value - Face value of a share of stock, set by the issuing company's board of directors.

Market value - Current price of a share of stock in the stock market.

Capital gain - Profit earned by selling a share of stock for more than its cost.

Book value - Value of a stock expressed as total stockholders' equity divided by the number of shares of common stock.

Blue chip stock - Common stock issued by a well-established company with a sound financial history and a stable pattern of dividend payouts.

Cumulative preferred stock - Preferred stock on which dividends not paid in the past must be paid to stockholders before dividends can be paid to common stockholders.

Stock exchange - Organization of individuals formed to provide an institutional setting in which stock can be traded.

Broker - Individual or organization who receives and executes buy and sell orders on behalf of other people in return for commissions.

Over-the-counter (OTC) market - Organization of securities dealers formed to trade stock outside the formal institutional setting of the organized stock exchanges.

Government bond - Bond issued by the federal government.

Municipal bond - Bond issued by a state or local government.

Corporate bond - Bond issued by a business as a source of long-term funding.

Registered bond - Bond bearing the name of the holder and registered with the issuing company.

Bearer (or coupon) bond - Bond requiring the holder to clip and submit a coupon to receive an interest payment.

Secured bond - Bond backed by pledges of assets to the bondholders.

Debenture - Unsecured bond for which no specific property is pledged as security.

Callable bond - Bond that may be called in and paid for by the issuer prior to its maturity date.

Sinking bond provision - Method for retiring bonds whereby the issuer puts enough money into a bank account to redeem the bonds at maturity.

Serial bond - Bond retired when the issuer redeems portions of the issue at different preset dates.

Convertible bond - Bond that can be retired by converting it to common stock.

Mutual fund - Company that pools investments from individuals and organizations to purchase a portfolio of stocks, bonds, and short-term securities.

No-load fund - Mutual fund in which investors pay no sales commissions when they buy in or sell out.

Load fund - Mutual fund in which investors are charged sales commissions when they buy in or sell out.

Futures contract - Agreement to purchase specified amounts of a commodity at a given price on a set future date.

Commodities market - Market in which futures contracts are traded.

Margin - Percentage of the total sales price that a buyer must put up to place an order for stock or for futures contracts.

Price-earnings ratio - Current price of a stock divided by the firm's current annual earnings per share.

Bid price - Price that an OTC broker pays for a share of stock.

Asked price - Price that an OTC broker charges for a share of stock.

Market index - Summary of price trends in a specific industry or the stock market as a whole.

Bull market - Period of upward-moving stock prices.

Bear market - Period of falling stock prices.

Dow Jones Industrial Average - Market index based on the prices for 30 of the largest industrial firms listed on the NYSE.

Standard & Poor's Composite Index - Market index based on the performance of 400 industrial firms, 40 utilities, 40 financial institutions, and 20 transportation companies.

Market order - Order to buy or sell a security at the market price prevailing at the time the order is placed.

Limit order - Order authorizing the purchase of a stock only if its price is equal to or less than a specified amount.

Stop order - Order authorizing the sale of a stock if its price falls to or below a specified level.

Round lot - Purchase or sale of stock in units of 100 shares.

Odd lot - Purchase or sale of stock in fractions of round lots.

Short sale - Stock sale in which investors borrow securities from their brokers to be sold and then replaced at a specified future date.

Program trading - Large purchase or sale of a group of stocks, often triggered by computerized trading programs that can be launched without human supervision or control.

Securities and Exchange Commission (SEC) - Federal agency that administers U.S. securities laws to protect the investing public and to maintain smoothly functioning markets.

Prospectus - Registration statement filed with the SEC before the issuance of a new security.

Insider trading - Illegal practice of using special knowledge about a firm for profit or gain.

Blue-sky laws - Laws requiring securities dealers to be licensed and registered with the states in which they do business.

TRUE-FALSE QUESTIONS

1. Although common and preferred stocks are considered to be securities, corporate bonds are not.

2. An investment banker is a financial specialist in the purchasing and selling of new securities.

3. Existing stocks and bonds are sold in the secondary securities market.

4. The current price of a share of stock in the stock market is referred to as its par value.

5. Bob Smith buys some common stock for $10 per share on May first, and then sells those same stocks on June first at $17 per share. Smith has experienced capital gains.

6. With cumulative preferred stock, any missed dividend payments must be paid as soon as the firm is able to do so.

7. The New York Stock Exchange is the largest stock exchange in the United States.

8. Bonds that are rated AAA are of higher grade than bonds rated Aaa.

9. For those persons holding registered bonds, interest payment requires the sending of a registered coupon to the bond issuer.

10. The most widely cited U.S. stock index is the Standard & Poor's Composite Index.

MULTIPLE CHOICE QUESTIONS

1. He or she is a financial specialist in purchasing and reselling new securities. What do we call such a person?

   a. financial manager
   b. investment banker
   c. broker
   d. stock dealer

2. Stock values are expressed in three ways. Which item below is NOT one of the three ways of expressing stock value?

   a. par value
   b. market value
   c. exchange value
   d. book value

3. You buy some common stock with a price per share of $22. Some time later, you sell the same stocks at a price per share of $29. Your "profit" from these two transactions is referred to as--

    a. capital gains
    b. exchange income
    c. broker's dilemma
    d. market value

4. Take the total value of stockholders' equity in a corporation and divide that figure by the number of shares outstanding. The result obtained is referred to as--

    a. dividends per share
    b. book value
    c. price per share
    d. earnings per share

5. With some issues of preferred stock, a missed dividend will be made up as soon as the corporation is able to do so. And until the missed dividend is paid, the corporation may not pay a penny to the common stockholders. Such a preferred issue is referred to as--

    a. participating
    b. pay warranty
    c. convertible
    d. cumulative

6. What happened to the Dow Jones Industrial Average following the assassination of President Kennedy on November 22, 1963?

    a. it was not affected
    b. it dropped more than 40 points
    c. the next trading day it bounced back with a large gain
    d. it actually rose slightly on the day of the shooting

7. With an average of 202 million shares changing hands each day at the New York Stock Exchange (NYSE), over _____ percent of all shares traded on U.S. exchanges are traded here at the NYSE. Pick a response below that best fills in the blank ·in the preceding sentence.

    a. ten
    b. thirty
    c. fifty
    d. seventy

8. The textbook tells us that about 4,000 stocks are listed on the organized stock exchanges. Roughly how many issues are traded in the over-the-counter (OTC) market?

   a. 2,000
   b. 5,000
   c. 17,000
   d. 28,000

9. Which of the phrases below best defines the class of securities known as junk bonds?

   a. bonds rated low by the rating services
   b. bonds that are in default
   c. bonds that pay very low interest
   d. bonds that aggressive investors generally ignore

10. There are some differences between a registered bond and a bearer bond. One of those differences is listed below. Select that difference.

   a. one makes use of coupons
   b. one matures
   c. one may be convertible
   d. one may be callable

11. A corporation may be required to put a certain amount of money into a special bank account. At the end of a certain number of years, the money will be sufficient to redeem bonds issued by the corporation. The action just described is referred to by the term--

   a. serial bond
   b. sinking fund
   c. plan of redemption
   d. delayed protraction

12. We call them "convertible bonds." Well, what are they convertible to?

   a. other bonds of the corporation
   b. preferred stock of the corporation
   c. common stock of the corporation
   d. limited membership on the board of directors

13. There are companies that pool investments from individuals and organizations in order to purchase a portfolio of stocks, bonds, and short-term securities. Such companies are typically called--

   a. brokers
   b. mutual funds
   c. credit unions
   d. savings clubs

14. When a person invests in the commodities market, he or she need not put up all the money necessary to make the full purchase. Similar arrangements exist in other markets, too. The small amount that must be paid at the time of purchase is referred to as--

   a. margin
   b. cash tender
   c. buyer's pool
   d. the stake

15. If you note in the financial section of a newspaper that your favorite common stock is up by 1/8, this means that the value of a share of that stock has increased by--

   a. 8 cents
   b. 1/8 of a cent
   c. 1/8 of a share
   d. 12.5 cents

16. On the stock market page, the notation "pf" may appear after the name of the company issuing the stock. According to the textbook, "pf" stands for--

   a. price falling
   b. profitable this month
   c. preferred
   d. premium fixed

17. Most dividends on corporate common stocks are paid on a quarterly basis. The amount of a stock's dividend is shown on the stock market page. The figure on that page reports the dividend on a basis that is--

   a. quarterly
   b. annual
   c. semiannual
   d. monthly

18. It is defined as a division of stock which gives stockholders a greater number of shares but which does not change each individual's proportionate share of ownership. Which of the responses below is the best fit with the definition that you have just read?

   a. stock dividend
   b. stock split
   c. bond conversion
   d. proxy fight

19. On the bond page, you will find listed right beside the name of each corporation that has issued a bond the following item of information--

    a.   whether convertible or not
    b.   closing price
    c.   current yield
    d.   year of maturity

20. If you sell a stock short, and you truly desire to make money on the deal, then you are hoping that the stock you sold short will--

    a.   drop in price
    b.   rise in price
    c.   remain very stable in price
    d.   experience a stock split

WRITING TO LEARN

1. Provide a full and illustrated explanation as to why stocks and bonds are referred to as "securities."

2. What is the difference between the primary securities market and the secondary securities market? Which market does the Dow Jones Industrial Average keep track of?

3. The textbook has provided three different ways to put a value on a share of stock. Explain these three ways. Which do you think is most important for a stock market investor? Least important?

4. Provide as many as you can of the differences between common stock and preferred stock. If dividends are really important to you, which would you prefer? Why?

5. Define cumulative preferred stock. Then, go on to set up an example of how the cumulative concept works.

6. Discuss the major American stock exchanges and be sure to treat the relative importance of each one to the investing public as well as to the general public.

7. What is the over-the-counter (OTC) market, and what is its impact in the overall scheme of financial markets? Give a general description of the types of companies whose stock will be found in the OTC.

8. Go back to inform yourself about NASDAQ. When you have done that, draw up a narrative sketch about how important NASDAQ can be around the world in the next millennium.

9. In complete argumentative detail, explain why you would or would NOT be willing to invest heavily in some junk bonds.

DISCUSSION OF BUSINESS CASE 18

The Marvel Comics yarn reiterates a previously-learned lesson and provides a new one. As for the old lesson, we see that a successful firm can never sit back and relax. This is because the environment surrounding the firm is in a constant state of change. To stay afloat, the firm must be constantly adapting. At least according to Barron's, Marvel was set to face some serious setbacks and there was no evidence available (to Barron's, at least) that Marvel was ready for them. The new lesson is that the press can be very powerful. Note how Marvel's stock dropped from $66 a share down to $54.625 just because of the Barron's story. This would say to us that being successful is not enough; you must give the press the impression that you are successful. Noting the power of the press, we are reminded how the press got itself in trouble some years ago and was accused of what amounted to illegal "insider trading." Here's how authorities alleged that it happened. There was a writer for a national financial newspaper whose job was to compose articles about how certain major companies were getting along financially. When the writer's editor informed him or her that a certain article would be appearing on a certain day, that writer would allegedly contact friends and say something like this: "My very complimentary article on the favorable financial condition of Purple Corporation will be appearing on Wednesday. Surely when the article hits, common stock of Purple will rise rapidly. So, what you want to do is buy up as much Purple common as you can before my article, and then watch the price jump. Sell the stock after my article has had effect, and you'll make a handsome profit. We can even share the profit." Avoiding the regulatory and legal matters that followed the revelation of the alleged operation, we may just say that it became very clear that the writer's articles definitely did have an impact on a stock's market performance. That makes sense, since it is psychological factors that account for much of the market's movement.

1. If you were Ronald Perelman of Marvel Comics, what would your reaction be to Barron's for printing that most unfavorable article?

2. Did the narrative give you any hints to the possibility that some of the Barron's story might have been flawed? Why or why not?

3. How much luck do you think Mr. Perelman of Marvel Comics would have in trying to get Barron's to do a follow-up story in which positive points about Marvel could be emphasized? Should Perelman turn to other newspapers for such a chance?

4. Compare and contrast the unfavorable Barron's article with a review of a new Broadway show that is terribly nasty and critical.

ANSWERS TO TRUE-FALSE QUESTIONS

1. F (p. 449)
2. T (p. 450)
3. T (p. 450-451)
4. F (p. 451)
5. T (p. 451)
6. T (p. 453)
7. T (p. 456)
8. F (p. 457)
9. F (p. 460)
10. F (p. 465)

ANSWERS TO MULTIPLE CHOICE QUESTIONS

1. b (p. 450)
2. c (p. 451)
3. a (p. 451)
4. b (p. 453)
5. d (p. 453)
6. c (p. 455)
7. c (p. 456)
8. d (p. 457)
9. a (p. 457)
10. a (p. 460)
11. b (p. 461)
12. c (p. 461)
13. b (p. 462)
14. a (p. 462-463)
15. d (p. 464)
16. c (p. 464)
17. b (p. 464)
18. b (p. 465)
19. d (p. 465)
20. a (p. 467)